Ecclesiastes

Finding Meaning in a
World of Passing Pursuits

BARNABAS PIPER

Lifeway Press®
Nashville, Tennessee

Editorial Team

Angel Prohaska
Production Editor

Jon Rodda
Art Director

Brett McIntosh
Content Editor

Tyler Quillet
Editorial Team Lead

Reid Patton
Content Editor

Joel Polk
Adult Discipleship Publisher

Published by Lifeway Press® • © 2022 Barnabas Piper

ISBN 978-1-0877-6302-6 • Item 005837453

Dewey decimal classification: 248.84
Subject headings: CHRISTIAN LIFE / HAPPINESS / BIBLE. O.T. ECCLESIASTES--STUDY AND TEACHING

To order additional copies of this resource, write to Lifeway Resources Customer Service; One Lifeway Plaza; Nashville, TN 37234; fax 615-251-5933; call toll free 800-458-2772; order online at Lifeway.com; or email orderentry@lifeway.com.

Printed in the United States of America

Adult Ministry Publishing • Lifeway Resources • One Lifeway Plaza • Nashville, TN 37234

Contents

About the Author

BARNABAS PIPER is an assistant pastor at Immanuel Church in Nashville and is the author or coauthor of several books and small group studies, including *The Pastor's Kid*, *Help My Unbelief*, and *Hoping for Happiness*. Prior to being called into ministry Barnabas worked in Christian publishing for almost 15 years. He co-hosts The Happy Rant podcast, writes regularly for He Reads Truth, and has contributed to numerous other websites and publications. Piper speaks regularly at churches, camps, and conferences around the country. He lives in the Nashville area with his wife and two daughters.

How to Use This Study

This Bible study book includes eight weeks
of content for group or individual study.

Reading Wisdom Literature

On the pages directly following this one, you will find a guide to understanding wisdom literature. This section is designed to give you helpful direction for understanding and processing the book of Ecclesiastes.

Group Sessions

Regardless of what day of the week your group meets, each week of content begins with the group session. Each group session uses the following format to facilitate simple yet meaningful interaction among group members, with God's Word, and with the video teaching from author Barnabas Piper.

START. This page includes questions to get the conversation started and to introduce the main topic of the session teaching.

WATCH. This section provides space for taking notes as participants watch the video. Codes to access the teaching videos are included with your purchase of this book and can be found on the insert located at the back of this book.

DISCUSS. This page includes questions and statements that guide the group to respond to Barnabas's teaching and to explore relevant biblical truth.

A NOTE ABOUT DOING THIS STUDY AS AN INDIVIDUAL. You may choose to do this study as an individual as opposed to participating in the group. If so, treat the group session and the associated teaching video as the first day of study for the week then proceed with the personal study portion.

Personal Study

Each week provides three opportunities for personal study—a guided reading plan and two days of Bible study.

GUIDED READING. This study covers the book of Ecclesiastes thematically. Each session includes a guided reading plan with several readings from Ecclesiastes and brief commentary. These readings could be done in one siting or across a whole week. These plans are designed to deepen your understanding of the book of Ecclesiastes and help you discern the themes it discusses.

PERSONAL BIBLE STUDIES. Additionally, the personal study section includes two three-page Bible studies. Each includes learning activities for individual engagement between group sessions. The personal study revisits stories, Scriptures, and themes introduced in the video teaching, so that participants can understand and apply them on a personal level.

Leader Guide

Lastly, in the back of this resource there is a leader guide included to help those leading others through this study. There you will find some tips for leading a small group as well as specific considerations for each session of study.

Reading Wisdom Literature

While the Bible is a single volume, it is composed of sixty-six individual books. Those books can be categorized into different genres: law, history/narrative, poetry, wisdom literature, prophecy, gospels, epistles, and apocalyptic. Don't let this overwhelm you! It's actually a beautiful depiction of God's creativity and care for His people. Each genre reveals something unique about God in both style and substance. Each genre draws readers to truth and the person of God in a distinct way, and we need them all.

We must also approach each genre differently. We can't read poetry like history or wisdom literature like epistles. We need to read them in their intended style so we can really see what God is revealing of Himself.

Ecclesiastes, Proverbs, and Job comprise the wisdom literature genre. The aim of wisdom literature is to help us grow in biblical wisdom (obviously). What is that? In short, it is living life with godly skill, thinking with the mind of God, and prioritizing or judging with godly priorities. These books deal in the substance of everyday life, and our goal in reading them is to learn how to faithfully walk with the Lord in all of life.

Here are a few pointers for reading wisdom literature to get the most out of it.

1. Remember that these are God's words as much as any other book of the Bible, even if they seem opaque or confusing sometimes. Wisdom literature reveals the mind, the priorities, the decision-making, and the character of God. While it may not have many propositional statements about God, all wisdom literature is essentially God telling us how He thinks.

2. Wisdom literature, especially proverbs, should be read as principles, not promises. We can find exceptions to every principle (e.g., if you work hard you will succeed). So we must read these books as principle truths rather than truths specific to every circumstance. Principles are true in general. And they are the way things ought to be.

3. Wisdom literature is often poetic, so it uses word pictures and vivid imagery. It is not to be read like a scientific or doctrinal work marked by linguistic precision. Rather, we are to consider: what is it evoking, what is it drawing out of our hearts? That is the aim of biblical wisdom, to transform the heart into alignment with God.

4. Ancient poetry often uses parallelism: stating truths in couplets that often seem at odds but that actually clarify and uphold one another. For example Proverbs 26:4-5 says, "Answer not a fool according to his folly, lest you be like him yourself. Answer a fool according to his folly, lest he be wise in his own eyes." Which is it? Remember that the aim is godly skill and discernment, so both are true and only wisdom can help us determine which is applicable and helpful in a given circumstance.

5. Because of poetic language and techniques like parallelism, we must be cautious about pulling a verse out of its context to prove a point or offer as a command. For example, consider Proverbs 26:4 again, "Answer not a fool according to his folly, lest you be like him yourself." Take that out of context and we lose the counterbalance of "Answer a fool according to his folly, lest he be wise in his own eyes." Context matters in all biblical interpretation, but it is especially significant when dealing with principles and evocative language.

6. Sometimes wisdom literature focuses on anti-wisdom (what the Bible calls foolishness) so that we can see both the consequences of defying God and the beauty of walking with Him. Ecclesiastes and Job do this. This means we must read them with an eye toward the greater reality of God's heart, God's desires, God's design, and God's priorities. Otherwise we can mistake a lengthy passage about anti-wisdom as prescriptive for our lives or as morally good.

7. All wisdom literature must be read in light of Genesis 1, God's good creation according to His perfect design, and in light of Genesis 3, the reality of sin and God's curse on the world that brought about the disordering and twisting of all things. Much of wisdom is seeing the good in the twisted and the twisted or sinful in the good. It is rarely so simple as labeling something "good" or "bad." Rather wisdom allows us to recognize the reflection of Genesis 1 and the marks of Genesis 3 in all aspects of life.

8. Remember that all wisdom is fulfilled and embodied in Christ. We cannot gain godly wisdom outside of life in Jesus. He is our means of wisdom through His saving work and the giving of His Holy Spirit. It is easy to think of "gaining wisdom" as something we do through discipline and rigor. And while we do strive for it, it is given by God through His Son.

Vanity Under the Sun

Start

Use this section to get the conversation started.

What types of books do you enjoy reading? What types of books do you tend to avoid?

What has your experience been reading Ecclesiastes before? What have you struggled with? What have you appreciated?

Ecclesiastes is a challenging book, one that doesn't even seem to fit in the Bible at first glance. In past reading of Ecclesiastes, you might have found yourself asking the question—what is this even doing in here? Ecclesiastes is wisdom literature like Proverbs and Job, but it seems to have a very different message than those books. Many of us read the book and can't quite figure out what the message is! We often treat it as one of those portions of Scripture reserved for checking boxes on a Bible reading plan, but not really for understanding.

Over the next eight sessions we're going to examine the broad themes of Ecclesiastes. In this session, we will be looking at the context of the book—vanity under the sun.

Watch

Take notes as you watch video session 1.

To access the teaching sessions,
use the instructions in the back
of your Bible study book.

Discuss

Use this section to guide your group discussion.

Read the opening verses of Ecclesiastes.

> *Vanity of vanities, says the Preacher,*
> *vanity of vanities! All is vanity.*
> **ECCLESIASTES 1:1-2**

These verses summarize the main theme of Ecclesiastes. How would you describe this theme in your own words?

Ecclesiastes is a profoundly realistic book. It invites us to confront the state of the world. The meaning of vanity in Ecclesiastes is something that is real and tangible, but not lasting—like an early morning fog. It also means that nothing functions the way it should and that nothing we experience will be as fulfilling as we hoped it would be. Ecclesiastes is warning us that we can't grasp onto anything in this life to fulfill us.

What have you hung your hopes on that has left you disappointed or disillusioned?

Even though we've been disappointed and disillusioned, why do we continue to hang our hopes on the things of this world?

Each of us has experienced disappointment and disillusionment because of work, family, injustice, comparison, or loss. Ecclesiastes addresses each of these challenges, but not with gentle words and saying "it'll be all right." We all know it's not always all right; the hurt is real. Instead it looks at reality the way the Bible defines it: fallen. We can't hang our hopes on anything in a fallen world because nothing is as it should be and nothing lasts.

How might a profoundly realistic perspective of our fallen world help us find happiness and purpose?

To understand Ecclesiastes, we have to recognize the context of the book, which we find in the opening chapter.

Read Ecclesiastes 1:9.

> *What has been is what will be,*
> *and what has been done is what will be done,*
> *and there is nothing new under the sun.*
> ECCLESIASTES 1:9

How does the phrase "under the sun" help us place the teaching of Ecclesiastes in context? How does this relate to the idea of vanity?

"Under the sun" is both a location and duration. It is a place and an amount of time. "Under the sun" describes the entire earth—everywhere the sun shines. It also refers to the fallen state of world under the curse of sin. Because of sin, nothing is as it should be and exists in a state of death and decay. Because of Jesus, we know that the state of the world "under the sun" is not permanent. Ecclesiastes paints a dark backdrop against which the reality of God's truth shines brightly.

How does looking to Jesus Christ shape our perspective on the life we live in a fallen world?

How does Jesus Christ give us hope in the fallen world that Ecclesiastes describes?

Ecclesiastes tells us that we look above and beyond the fallen world to find our hope. We look to Jesus Christ. And in doing so, we find out how we can actually find enjoyment and purpose and fulfillment in this world.

Close your time together with prayer.

Personal Study 1

Guided Reading

Read the following sections of Ecclesiastes to gain a
deeper appreciation for the context of the book.

ECCLESIASTES 1:1-15

This is a sweeping, broad introduction to the book of Ecclesiastes. It sets the stage
and context for what follows. Most importantly it introduces the concept of "all is vanity
under the sun," a lens through which the rest of the book must be read to make sense.

ECCLESIASTES 3:1-8

There is a time for everything under the sun; this is a characteristic of a fallen world.
It doesn't mean everything is good or as it should be, but simply that we live in
world marked by the goodness of God (life, healing, laughter, embracing, loving)
and the fallenness of sin (Genesis 3). So there is a time for pain, death, and loss
during this life as well. We are supposed to feel the tension in these verses as the
author juxtaposes the pleasant with the unpleasant.

ECCLESIASTES 3:19-22

Under the sun we are all marked by the same fate; all is vanity. Does that mean life is
not worth living or that we are of no greater value than the "beasts"? No. It means we
were not made to live "under the sun" but for a different hope and reality.

ECCLESIASTES 8:14-17

These verses highlight the mystery and confusion of life under the sun. Things do
not go the way they are supposed to—the righteous are rewarded as if they are
wicked and vice versa. This too is vanity because it is unsatisfying and unfulfilling.
Under the sun we are unable to understand or clearly see the ways of God and how
He is working, and this causes frustration and confusion. But verse 15 again lifts our
eyes away from bleak hopelessness. It points out that there is hope and joy in the
midst of this vain, confusing life.

ECCLESIASTES 11:8

A stark reminder that we are all mortal, that our days under the sun are numbered. But rather than finding this depressing, the verse points us to rejoicing and gratitude. The implication is that life is a gift, something from God to be treasured. So despite the fact that "all that comes is vanity" (nothing in this life lasts) we are to rejoice in what God does give.

ECCLESIASTES 12:7-8

A final reiteration of the temporal nature of all things, but not a passive one. Verse 7 points out that the spirit returns to God who gave it. It is pointing out that our lives are created by God, gifts from God. So yes, life on earth is "vain" and fleeting, but that does not change the reality that it is God-given.

Notes

Personal Study 2

All is Vanity

Read the opening words of Ecclesiastes.

The words of the Preacher, the son of David, king in Jerusalem.

Vanity of vanities, says the Preacher,
   vanity of vanities! All is vanity.
ECCLESIASTES 1:1-2

Define the word vanity.

I live in middle Tennessee, near Nashville, and it's not uncommon for us to have early morning fog. Sometimes it's so thick I can't see but a few feet in front of my car. When fog like this happens it's eerie, beautiful, and demands that I drive very cautiously.

I love bonfires in the fall. Sitting around with friends and family, talking and laughing, making s'mores, sipping drinks—it's the best . . . until the smoke blows my way. (And we all know that smoke follows us as we move around the fire too.) It stings my eyes, makes me cough, and generally interrupts an otherwise wonderful time.

My route to drop my kids off at school takes me by a big lake. Sometimes when the weather is calm and it has just started to turn cold a mist sits on the lake, just above the water. It catches the early morning sun and looks ethereal and peaceful. Photos never do it justice.

What do fog, smoke, and mist have in common? They are all real, visible, and affect us. And then they are gone. The fog and the mist blow away with a breeze or a temperature change. The smoke is gone on the wind, or when dry wood is added to the fire. This is a picture of what "vanity" means in Ecclesiastes.

What do the images of fog, smoke, or mist teach you about what "vanity" means in Ecclesiastes?

We often think of vanity as a mirror, or as a trait of someone who really likes to look at himself in that mirror. ("He's so vain, always thinking about his appearance.") Or maybe we think of it in terms of purpose. A vain effort is a pointless one and comes to nothing. Vain hopes are useless, a waste of time because they won't come true.

In Ecclesiastes vanity means something else. It means a vapor, something temporal and passing, something there and gone. And ultimately this means it is something unfulfilling, something that does not satisfy our longings.

What are things in your life you have counted on to fulfill you but that do not satisfy?

What did Solomon (the author of Ecclesiastes) mean when he used this word? How is the way he used this word different than the way we often use it?

Understanding vanity is the key to understanding Ecclesiastes. When you read the opening words of the book it appears the preacher is extraordinarily pessimistic, saying that life is pointless. It could be read as "Nothing is worth anything." But we have to ask ourselves, "Does understanding vanity that way square with the rest of the Bible?"

Consider what you know about the rest of the Bible; is Ecclesiastes saying "nothing is worth anything"? What else might "all is vanity" mean?

To understand what this means we need to consider two things: first, the whole of Scripture and second, the definition I gave for "vanity" a couple paragraphs ago.

When we think of God's good creation (Genesis 1), God's promises, God's covenant with His people, God sending Jesus to rescue and redeem lost sinners like us, and the promise of Jesus's return, we know this cannot mean that life is pointless and not worth living. The whole Bible proclaims the value of living with God. So it must mean something else.

What Bible passages come to mind (stories, promises, teaching) that display the value and goodness of life with God?

So let's consider the definition of "vanity" I gave earlier: a vapor, something temporal and passing, something there and gone—something unfulfilling, something that does not satisfy our longings. This means that Ecclesiastes is not saying that life is worthless, but that nothing in this life ultimately satisfies. It isn't saying life is pointless, but that everything good in this life does not last and does not wholly fulfill us. While this isn't exactly joyous, it is quite different than a perspective that would make us give up on life and happiness.

How have you experienced the kind of "vanity" Ecclesiastes describes?

Ecclesiastes is not robbing us of hope. Rather, it is uprooting us from false hope and replanting us where true hope and happiness exist. Compelling us to lift our eyes to a different reality far better than the passing vapor of meaning we find in this life.

By erasing false or shallow hope, what is Ecclesiastes pointing us to instead?

In the next study we will look closely at a phrase Ecclesiastes uses time and again: "under the sun" (1:9). This is a clue as to both the context for why "all is vanity" and to where true, lasting happiness and fulfillment exist.

Personal Study 3

Under the Sun

A few years ago I had a minor surgery done. The doctor told me they weren't going to put me fully under anesthesia, but that local anesthetics wouldn't be strong enough. So they did what they called "twilight anesthesia," which means placing me in a state somewhere between awake and asleep. I have some vague, passing memories of moments throughout the surgery, but it mostly felt foggy and surreal.

If you are a sports fan, you've likely heard an older player described as "in the twilight of his career." It refers to those last few seasons when he is in decline but still has some game left. He can produce here and there, but the end is near.

Read Ecclesiastes 1:9.

What has been is what will be,
and what has been done is what will be done,
and there is nothing new under the sun.
ECCLESIASTES 1:9

This verse introduces the phrase "under the sun." At first it's easy to read right past this little phrase and think nothing of it, but we can't do that. "Under the sun" is the context for the whole book of Ecclesiastes. It is used in some form over twenty times throughout the book as a reminder of the context, setting, and truths being written.

When you read "under the sun" what do you think it means?
What is the Bible trying to communicate?

What do anesthesia, old athletes, and "under the sun" have to do with each other? Twilight. Under the sun is not primarily a geographic description as much as it is a description of time and clarity, of lifespan and understanding. It's a duration more than a location. "Under the sun" is the Solomon's way of describing how we exist as human beings in a fallen world that we have entered into and will one day pass away from.

Why is it significant that "under the sun" primarily describes time/lifespan and clarity/understanding? What is Ecclesiastes trying to focus our attention on?

Just as twilight anesthesia was foggy, disconnected, and sleepy, so life "under the sun" is foggy and disconnected from God's perfect reality. We all feel that disconnect and experience it in disappointment and lack of fulfillment. We instinctively agree with Ecclesiastes that all is vanity under the sun. Everything is in the twilight of its lifespan, like the careers of those football players. It all passes away.

"Under the sun" has a geographic aspect to it as well; specifically it relates to the lives we lead during our time on earth. In the movie, *The Lion King* (cartoon edition, i.e. the good edition) Mufasa takes his son, Simba, up to Pride Rock and declares "Everything the light touches is our kingdom." The same is true for our temporal, twilight realities—everywhere the sun rises and sets is the kingdom marked by vanity. Vanity is the state of being for the whole earth.

Reflect on the comprehensive nature of "under the sun." It defines our location (on earth), our time (lifespan), and our understanding (foggy, incomplete). Why is life this way? What does the Bible have to say elsewhere to help you understand?

What Ecclesiastes is describing is the day-to-day, lived-out effects of the curse of Genesis 3. In Genesis 3, Adam and Eve rebelled against God by deciding they wanted to function as their own gods, to have His knowledge and make their own decisions about what was best for them. As a consequence, God marked the world with a curse that touches every aspect of every part of life. Instead of perfect union and joyous relationship with Him, the world became marked by vanity under the sun—everything passes and fails to fulfill.

Read Genesis 3:14-19 and consider how the curses of sin define and describe life "under the sun."

The curse is a separation from God, a breaking of relationship both in physical creation and in our souls. We are "under the sun," shaped by mortality, entropy (the tendency toward decay and decline), and inertia (the tendency toward doing nothing and remaining unchanged). As you consider your mortality, don't make it an intellectual exercise. The curse is a profound biblical reality that each of us feels in our bones and carries the weight of in our hearts. We know the disappointment and grief when nothing satisfies as we hoped it would, either because it's defective or short-lived. We feel the strain in maintaining a close relationship with God, often feeling like He is far away. If we're honest, we go through life with the sense that things are not as they ought to be.

> **When have you experienced the disappointment, grief, and pain of life "under the sun"? How is this feeling related to our separation from God?**

The writer of Ecclesiastes is not fatalistic or a doomsayer. He is not wallowing in the misery of life nor is he a nihilistic screenwriter giving us an empty, depressing biopic. In the same way that he seeks to uproot false hopes by pointing out vanity, he seeks to lift our eyes to a different reality by describing life "under the sun." He is pointing us to something better, a life that could be described as "above the sun." Remember, Ecclesiastes is wisdom literature. That means it is guiding us to see things the way God sees them and to connect to His heart, His desires, and His way of living.

> **How does the bleak background of life under the sun help us see the goodness and beauty of walking with God in this life?**

Reading and studying Ecclesiastes in the context of vanity under the sun is vital for our understanding. You must keep it in mind and look for it throughout the verses of this dense book. It will keep you connected to God's heart in this book—an invitation to look above the sun to the light and joy of life with Him. That perspective will allow us to live the life he has given us under the sun with peace, wisdom, and satisfaction.

> **How does the promise of a reality "above the sun" lift your heart?**

Wisdom

Start

Use this section to get the conversation started.

Sometimes when you're reading or studying something you get that "record scratch" moment—the one where everything screeches to a halt and you have to reconsider what you've thought up to that point. In Ecclesiastes that happens right up front. It starts with the hard stuff. The author wanted to make really clear what the framework for this book is: all is vanity under the sun.

> **How did the concept of "all is vanity" land on you as you studied it last session? Did it ring true? Was it depressing or burdensome? Explain.**

> **How did the framework of "under the sun" offer clarity in understanding "all is vanity"? How did it help you see our current, fallen reality versus the promise of a coming, perfect reality with God?**

Solomon understood that most of us aren't great at taking big concepts and applying them specifically to life. Usually the concepts are too big or too disconnected from day-to-day life for us to work it out. So he begins to walk readers through specific areas of life that are vain under the sun.

He picks areas of life we value highly, things we look at as good and worth investing in (and, in fact, they are). So he is challenging our sensibilities and our values. He is showing that even our thinking about how to value good things is not quite right and that we need a new understanding from God.

The next four sessions will each focus on one of these areas of life. This session we'll explore Ecclesiastes' teaching on wisdom—specifically on the vanity of wisdom.

Watch

Take notes as you watch video session 2.

To access the teaching sessions, use the instructions in the back of your Bible study book.

Discuss

Use this section to guide your group discussion.

If saying that wisdom is vain sounds odd to you, good. Ecclesiastes ought to make us raise an eyebrow. Part of its purpose is to shake us out of a stupor that keeps us meandering through life, going from one pursuit to the next without really seeing God's truth. Ecclesiastes wants us to remember that "Whatever your hand finds to do, do it with your might" (9:10). That means pursuing life with thoughtfulness and clarity, not just blind effort.

> **Biblical wisdom can be defined as "living life with godly skill, thinking with the mind of God, and prioritizing or judging with godly priorities." Why is this kind of wisdom necessary for living a godly life?**
>
> **Consider the definition of vanity and the context of "under the sun" we saw last session. How might wisdom be vain? What is Ecclesiastes trying to show us about even godly wisdom?**

When thinking about what Ecclesiastes is trying to teach us, we need to remember the way it uses the term "vanity" and understand the sweeping context of "under the sun" that we discussed last session. Ecclesiastes seeks to adjust our perspective, even on truly good and valuable things. Remember, the book began with "all is vanity," not just "shallow things are vanity" or "immoral things are vanity." Even good things pass away during this life under the sun. So Ecclesiastes is not saying wisdom is a waste of time but rather that even godly wisdom has limits in this fallen world.

> **Where do you encounter the limits of godly wisdom, in your own life or in general?**

Let's consider some of these limitations by posing some questions. We don't need to answer all of these but rather to find the thread that runs through them.

- *What is the name of your great great grandmother?*
- *Why hasn't a cure for all kinds of cancer been developed?*
- *Who can solve the flaws in our justice system and overcrowding in our prisons?*

- *What inspired the sentence "Those who forget history are doomed to repeat it"?*
- *Why do some of us only learn lessons by failure rather than through good advice?*
- *Why do the rich get richer while global poverty remains a problem?*

What is the thread in these questions? What do they teach us about wisdom?

Wisdom has limits, not because of a flaw in wisdom but because of brokenness in the world. Wise people pass away and we forget them and their wisdom, almost like they never existed. Wisdom falls into the abyss between generations so that we fail to learn from those who came before us, and therefore repeat the same mistakes they made. The world is full of sin and evil and things are not as they are supposed to be. We often resist godly wisdom, and people with godly wisdom are not able to solve all the world's problems. Wisdom is vain because it is subject to the same fallenness of everything else under the sun.

Given this blunt assessment of wisdom in a fallen world, in what sense is wisdom worth pursuing?

All the vanity and shortcomings of wisdom are disappointing and heartbreaking. All the problems wisdom can't solve in this life are overwhelming. Remember, though, Ecclesiastes is not here to tell us how terrible life is or how hopeless. It is here to change our perspective and lift our eyes. If wisdom under the sun cannot make the world right there must be a different solution, a different hope. It must be something or someone infinitely greater than all the wisdom in the history of the world.

How does Ecclesiastes' teaching on wisdom make you reconsider how much hope you put in human wisdom?

What does this teaching about the vanity of wisdom show us about where true hope lies?

Close your time together with prayer.

Personal Study 1
Guided Reading

During the next week read the following verses to gain a deeper appreciation for what Ecclesiastes teaches about wisdom.

ECCLESIASTES 1:12-18

Solomon, the author of Ecclesiastes and one of the wisest men who ever lived, describes his pursuit of wisdom and the discovery that it is vain because of the fallen condition of mankind.

ECCLESIASTES 2:12-17

These verses weigh the value of wisdom under the sun. Wisdom brings light to a dark world, but it also passes away. And they highlight that all is vanity because the same fate befalls everyone, wise or foolish.

ECCLESIASTES 7:1-29

The first 13 verses of chapter 7 are proverbs, highlighting the merits of wisdom over foolishness but also the limitations of wisdom. The final portion of the chapter explores the confusion and foolishness of how the world works (the thriving of the wicked, the struggling of the righteous, etc.) but also the goodness of wisdom in the midst. It reads a little bit like a seesaw, back and forth between vanity and goodness.

ECCLESIASTES 8:14-17

These verses highlight the benefit of finding joy in this life and that seeking to understand all God is doing is beyond our understanding. It is an acknowledgment of God's sovereignty and a reminder to trust in Him even if life is beyond our understanding.

ECCLESIASTES 9:11-18

This passage acknowledges the confusion and foolishness of life but presents wisdom as clearly the best option. Essentially it says, "Despite the fact that life is a mess and doesn't make sense, wisdom is profoundly better than any other option and offers our only hope."

ECCLESIASTES 10:1-20

This chapter is composed of proverbs that present the emptiness of earthly assumptions and pursuits while highlighting the good of wisdom in the midst of that bleakness. It is aimed at adjusting our perspective on the things we might instinctively put our hopes in to the goodness of godly wisdom.

ECCLESIASTES 12:9-14

These final words of Ecclesiastes declare the source of true wisdom (God) and that it is the only reliable thing in the world. They lift our attention and perspective from the confusion of life under the sun to the clarity of life with God above the sun.

Notes

Personal Study 2

Wisdom Under the Sun

What do you understand "wisdom" to mean? How does the broader culture define it?

We know wisdom is more than a collection of knowledge; after all, any library or hard drive is a collection of information and we'd never call them "wise." (Not to mention the internet, home of almost all information and possibly the most foolish place on earth too.) So instead we turn to terms like smart, clever, savvy, knowledgeable, understanding, or discerning to define wisdom. But we also know wisdom is more than any single one of these terms, so we'd likely combine a few in an attempt to define it.

We also attempt to define wisdom by what it is capable of doing. Wisdom can solve problems. Wisdom understands people. Wisdom knows a lot of stuff. Wisdom knows what to do in hard situations. Wisdom is experienced and has seen it all. Ecclesiastes, on the other hand, seems to be emphasizing what wisdom can't do.

Read the following verses and underline what they teach about the limits of wisdom.

For in much wisdom is much vexation, and he who increases knowledge increases sorrow.
ECCLESIASTES 1:18

The wise person has his eyes in his head, but the fool walks in darkness. And yet I perceived that the same event happens to all of them.
ECCLESIASTES 2:14

For of the wise as of the fool there is no enduring remembrance, seeing that in the days to come all will have been long forgotten.
ECCLESIASTES 2:16

When I applied my heart to know wisdom, and to see the business that is done on earth, how neither day nor night do one's eyes see sleep, then I saw all the work of God, that man cannot find out the work that is done under the sun. However much man may toil in seeking, he will not find it out. Even though a wise man claims to know, he cannot find it out.
ECCLESIASTES 8:16–17

*But I say that wisdom is better than might, though the poor man's
wisdom is despised and his words are not heard.*
ECCLESIASTES 9:16

*The words of the wise are like goads, and like nails firmly fixed are
the collected sayings; they are given by one Shepherd.*
ECCLESIASTES 12:11

Wisdom cannot bring peace (1:18), fend off mortality (2:14), endure (2:16), give us understanding of the mind or work of God (8:16-17), earn us honor (9:16), or own our hearts and minds (12:11).

Beyond these verses, Chapter 7 paints a picture of wisdom being good, but not being able to deliver enduring happiness or peace. It speaks of wise people being diminished and passing away while fools prosper. Chapter 10 contrasts wisdom with foolishness, and wisdom absolutely comes out ahead. But it doesn't eradicate foolishness; that plague still affects us all.

**What do these verses, these limitations of wisdom, stir in your heart?
How do they change your understanding of wisdom?**

**What do these verses tell us about what foolishness means? What do they
show us about the pervasiveness of foolishness in the world?**

The thread that runs through these verses is not how weak and worthless wisdom is. Rather, it is that wisdom, no matter if it is the man-centered earthly definition (knowledge, savvy, skill, experience) or the deeper biblical definition (godly skill, values, and understanding), cannot solve the world's problems. The vanity of wisdom is not its lack of value or goodness but its limited effectiveness in a world marked by sin and death. Ecclesiastes is telling us that wisdom is good, essential, and valuable. And it is not enough to repair all that is broken and right all that is wrong.

Remember, vanity means a vapor. Wisdom, no matter how good and how real, passes away. It is there and then it isn't. Its effects are seen and felt until they are gone like mist.

Ecclesiastes

How have you seen and felt the vanity of wisdom? How have you experienced the limitations of wisdom in a broken world?

If wisdom is vain, what is our hope under the sun? What can we turn to that will make a difference and make things right?

Before we fall prey to the temptation of thinking that wisdom is, in fact, pointless, remember Ecclesiastes 12:11 from the previous page. Who gave wisdom? One Shepherd. This means wisdom is from God, so no matter how frustrated we get by what it cannot resolve in this world we still hold fast to wisdom because no word of God will return void but will accomplish what He intends (Isaiah 55:11). And what does God intend?

Why is Ecclesiastes so intent on showing the vanity of wisdom?

Ecclesiastes shows us that we cannot grasp all that God is doing on earth (8:16-17) and tells us that we cannot understand the scope of all God's work throughout history (3:11). But, while we cannot understand all God intends, we do know that His Word is meant to lift our eyes and hearts to Him in trust. It is a revelation of who He is, so the frustration and inadequacy we feel because our wisdom cannot fix life under the sun are not meant to leave us defeated but to incline us to depend on God. They are meant to show us that we need a greater wisdom—godly skill, values, and understanding that are so magnificent and so perfect that they can repair all that is broken.

What wisdom under the sun, even godly wisdom, cannot do, Christ can. In the next study we will explore the wisdom of Christ and how it shapes our lives under the sun. But as we close this study, reflect on the limits of wisdom to resolve all that is broken in the world and in your life. And reflect on our need for Jesus. Because that is what Ecclesiastes intends for us to see—not hopelessness, not meaninglessness, but limitations and needs that can only be met by a perfect Savior.

Personal Study 3
The Goodness of Wisdom

Ecclesiastes functions as a sort of case study in wisdom. We saw already that wisdom is not merely knowing a lot or being able to cleverly solve problems or understand complex issues. Much of wisdom is the ability to hold multiple ideas in tension. Rather than simplistic, black-and-white thinking where we create binaries, wisdom considers multiple options and weighs the merits of each. And this is exactly what Ecclesiastes is doing.

How is Ecclesiastes exemplifying wisdom? Where do we see it weighing ideas and considering values rather than simply declaring something "good" or "bad"?

In the previous study we looked at the vanity of wisdom. Verse after verse highlighted the limitations of wisdom and all that it cannot accomplish under the sun. This is one reality that must be considered. But we must also consider what Ecclesiastes declares about the goodness of wisdom.

Read the following verses, taking note of what they teach about wisdom.

What is crooked cannot be made straight, and what is lacking cannot be counted.
ECCLESIASTES 1:15

For in much wisdom is much vexation, and he who increases knowledge increases sorrow.
ECCLESIASTES 1:18

The wise person has his eyes in his head, but the fool walks in darkness. And yet I perceived that the same event happens to all of them.
ECCLESIASTES 2:14

Wisdom gives strength to the wise man more than ten rulers who are in a city.
ECCLESIASTES 7:19

Ecclesiastes

Wisdom helps us open our eyes to "crookedness" and "vexation" in order to navigate brokenness (1:15 and 1:18). Wisdom keeps us from adding to our brokenness (2:14). It helps us bear the burdens of life (7:19). Let's continue reading from Ecclesiastes.

> *But I say that wisdom is better than might, though the poor man's wisdom is despised and his words are not heard. The words of the wise heard in quiet are better than the shouting of a ruler among fools. Wisdom is better than weapons of war, but one sinner destroys much good.*
> **ECCLESIASTES 9:16-18**

> *A wise man's heart inclines him to the right, but a fool's heart to the left.*
> **ECCLESIASTES 10:2**

> *The words of a wise man's mouth win him favor, but the lips of a fool consume him.*
> **ECCLESIASTES 10:12**

> *The words of the wise are like goads, and like nails firmly fixed are the collected sayings; they are given by one Shepherd.*
> **ECCLESIASTES 12:11**

Ecclesiastes teaches that wisdom is of greater value than status and will do more good, because destruction and conflict can be avoided by wisdom (9:16-18). Wisdom walks with the Lord and away from destruction and foolishness which in Scripture is rebellion against God (10:2). In these verses, we also see, that as a principle, speaking wisely will be well-received and trusted (10:12). Ultimately these verses declare wisdom from God to be trustworthy, unchanging, and the whole of what we need to navigate life under the sun (12:11-12).

How do you reconcile the vanity of wisdom with the goodness of wisdom as presented in the same book of the Bible, and sometimes within the very same verses?

Ecclesiastes is an exercise in wisdom because it demands that we hold the vanity of wisdom and the goodness of wisdom in tension. These realities seem irreconcilable at first. How can something that is unable to solve the woes of this life be the very thing we need to navigate this life under the sun? The answer, as Ecclesiastes always wants us to remember, lies above the sun.

Reflect for a moment on the reality of "under the sun." How does this define the limits of wisdom? How does reality "above the sun" expand our understanding and help make sense out of the tensions?

Consider Paul's words about Jesus.

> And because of him you are in Christ Jesus, who became to us wisdom from God, righteousness and sanctification and redemption.
> **1 CORINTHIANS 1:30**

In what ways is Jesus our wisdom? What do you think this means?

The incarnation of Jesus was the embodiment of godly wisdom entering life under the sun. He became wisdom for us.

Jesus was the perfect example of wisdom. He did all things with godly skill, insight, and values. Of course, we cannot perfectly follow his example because we are sinners. So Jesus also provided a means to wisdom for us. His death on the cross made a way for us to be in relationship with God by making us right with God so that we have access to life above the sun. Furthermore, Christ gave the Holy Spirit to all who believe as a helper and teacher, providing a means for us to grow in godly wisdom while we live under the sun.

In His infinite goodness, Jesus wasn't finished there. He promised that He would one day "wipe away every tear from their eyes, and death shall be no more, neither shall there be mourning, nor crying, nor pain anymore, for the former things have passed away" and that he would make "all things new" (Revelation 21:4-5). Even as we feel the vanity of wisdom under the sun, it is not for naught. All godly wisdom points to Jesus and the restoration and salvation He offers. Are we able to fix the world's problems? No. Can we right all the wrongs and solve all the injustice and pain? No. But He can, and He will, because Jesus is the perfect wisdom of God.

What does trusting in the wisdom of Jesus and walking in the wisdom of Jesus look like for you?

WEEK 3

Work

Start

Use this section to get the conversation started.

Picture a funnel. That is sort of how we are studying Ecclesiastes. We began at the wide end of the funnel, with the framework and reality of vanity under the sun. This reality of vanity covers everything in this life and is the context for all that follows. Then we went narrower by focusing on wisdom. But wisdom is still a broad category, touching every area of life in some way, because wisdom is how we think and value and make decisions about all the other stuff.

What stood out to you about wisdom from Ecclesiastes? What did you learn or how did your perspective change?

In the next three sessions we are going to get even narrower, focusing on what Ecclesiastes has to say about particular aspects of life. In this session we are going to focus on work.

How does work shape your life, family, and direction?

How much of your life and energy is devoted to work?

The wisdom literature of the Bible intends to guide us through the real stuff of life, not just theories. Work is a significant theme in Ecclesiastes for this very reason: we spend most of our waking hours doing it. Since work holds such a prominent place in our lives, Scripture has some things to tell us about how to think about it, how to approach it, how to value it, and even how to rest from it.

Watch

Take notes as you watch video session 3.

To access the teaching sessions,
use the instructions in the back
of your Bible study book.

Discuss

Use this section to guide your group discussion.

What place does work hold in your life? What do you expect out of your work or want it to do for you?

We spend the majority of our waking adult lives working (and if not the majority of our time, at least the majority of our energy). We go to school to get degrees to get good jobs. Once we get a job we begin scoping out how to advance either by promotion or new opportunities. We make difficult value decisions about relationships and family based on work.

What kinds of questions do we ask in relation to our work? What do these questions teach us about the space work occupies in our lives?

Work affects many of life's most important decisions. We ask questions such as, *Am I in a position to get married based on my career path? Can we afford to have kids based on how much money we earn? Should I quit work to stay at home with the kids or try to keep working full time? Would it be good or harmful for my family if we move across the country for a new job opportunity? Should I take the risk of changing careers altogether?* Work shapes the direction of our lives.

Ecclesiastes frequently describes work using the word "toil." How should this shape how we define "work"? What else in life fits in the category of toil beyond our careers?

Ecclesiastes is not just talking about employment and careers. It is talking about the toil and effort we put in to life to make it all work—the work it takes to build a life. Everything from education to church to parenting to managing finances to caring for a home to developing hobbies and on and on. We strive to piece together a mean-ingful, comfortable life for ourselves and our families. All of it is toil, even if we love it. And in the ultimate sense all of it is vanity.

How have you experienced the vanity of toil? What does that feel like?

Is Ecclesiastes saying all that effort to build a meaningful life is pointless? Not at all. I am saying, because Ecclesiastes says it, that it is not where ultimate identity and satisfaction are found. Not in achieving the apex of a career, not in building a serene home life, not in terminal degrees, and not in anything else we master by intellectual rigor, sweat of the brow, and dirt under the fingernails. All is vanity under the sun, all things pass away, including the fruits of your labors.

> **What should this tell us about the place of work in our lives?**
> **What should it tell us about where we place our hopes for satisfaction, identity, and fulfillment?**
>
> **If work does not fulfill us and does not give us identity, what does it do for us, and how should we approach it?**

Ecclesiastes offers a profoundly un-American perspective. We love being builders and believing that what we do will be remembered. But Ecclesiastes has the final word (it is God's Word, after all) and reminds us that our hope and identity are not in our accomplishments or skills. And it leaves us with this refrain, repeated several times throughout the book: "everyone should eat and drink and take pleasure in all [your] toil—this is God's gift to man" (2:24; 3:13; 5:18; 8:15). Again Ecclesiastes is adjusting our perspective away from that humanistic, "under the sun" shallowness we are so prone to and putting our eyes on what God is doing and what He wants for us. It tells us what not to expect from all our toil, but also what God gives us through it.

> **How do you think we should view our work in light of what we've learned about vanity and life under the sun?**

Close your time together with prayer.

Personal Study 1
Guided Reading

During the next week read the following verses to gain a deeper appreciation for what Ecclesiastes teaches about work.

ECCLESIASTES 1:3

This verse offers a clue as to the importance of considering our work. It is at the very front of the book, and it puts the question to the reader: what do we have to gain from all this effort?

ECCLESIASTES 2:18-26

These verses specifically highlight the vanity of work. We give our best energy to toil, and it will be passed on to someone else. We have little or no control over what will become of it. Not only this, we toil all our days with no reprieve, so it is all effort for uncertain outcomes. But these verses conclude with a refrain that appears throughout Ecclesiastes: eat, drink, and enjoy your work, for it is from God.

ECCLESIASTES 3:13,22

The refrain is repeated: eat, drink, and find joy in your toil. But this time Ecclesiastes emphasizes that this is a gift from God. It is also called our "lot," which means something like our inheritance, or the portion given to us.

ECCLESIASTES 4:4-6

These verses highlight a significant pitfall in our pursuit of success and excellence: all our skill and growth comes from envy. We improve at work because we want to catch up to someone else or be better than someone else. So work lends itself to pride, jealousy, and idolatry. As a countermeasure we are directed to "a handful of quietness" instead of "two handfuls of toil," meaning rest and taking a step back from work is much better than endless striving.

ECCLESIASTES 9:10

This verse tells us how we should work and why we should do so. We work with everything we have because this life is short. And this exhortation applies to more than just work. We should love, befriend, rest, play, and everything else with all our might because this life under the sun is our chance at doing so.

Notes

Personal Study 2

The Vanity of Work

Living in the southeastern United States, college football is a big deal here. On Saturdays in the fall it seems like everyone is decked out in their team's colors—Tennessee orange, Georgia red, Alabama crimson. People identify as part of their respective tribe. Their happiness, well-being, and sense of identity rise and fall with the success of their team. And there is even a sense of superiority among the fans of good teams and inferiority (or defensiveness) among the fans of struggling teams. We do the same thing with our work.

List some ways we seek identity and fulfillment through our work.

We identify as a teacher, pastor, parent, doctor, salesman, musician, builder, or student. We wear the "jersey" of our jobs, at least if it's a job with enough status and we're good enough at it. Our happiness rises and falls with the success of our industry, our relationships with co-workers, and the value of our work itself. We even judge others on their jobs, either as inferior or superior based on the perceived status of their position. This all says something, a lot actually, about the expectations we place on work.

Read Ecclesiastes 2:18-26 and 4:4-6.

Why do we try to derive so much personal value from work (and gauge the value of others by their work)?

What specific desires do you have for your work? What do you want it to deliver to you? Or what do you want to accomplish through it?

We approach work with the hope that it will fulfill us. We want satisfaction in our work, using our skills to do something meaningful that pays well so we have financial security. We want to enjoy our work and be proud of it, we want our efforts to really matter, and if we can't have those we at least want a fat paycheck. We tend to have the expectation that we'll "arrive" at a place of professional satisfaction at some point, maybe in the next job, the next promotion, or the next opportunity we pursue. And we want to leave behind a legacy of something more than just a financial inheritance for our kids and grandkids.

How do these hopes for satisfaction stack up against what Ecclesiastes says about work?

What are the pitfalls of banking on so much in our work?

Ecclesiastes describes a different reality for work. It paints a picture of endless toil and weariness, something we feel deeply. It addresses the wealth that is earned and how that creates inequity (more on wealth in the next session). And it even says that "all skill in work comes from a man's envy of his neighbor" (4:4). So under the sun, the pursuit of success in work is driven, at least in part, by jealousy and idolatry. While we may want good to come from our work, we don't have pure motives in our pursuits. We want what we don't have, whether that be money, skill, or happiness, and we expect work to deliver it.

What kind of lasting impact do you hope to make through your work? What do you hope to leave behind?

Ecclesiastes

Here again we run into "vanity and striving after the wind." Ecclesiastes is reflecting the reality of Genesis:

> *"By the sweat of your face*
> *you shall eat bread,*
> *till you return to the ground,*
> *for out of it you were taken;*
> *for you are dust,*
> *and to dust you shall return."*
> **GENESIS 3:19**

Work, it says, cannot fulfill us in this broken world. This side of heaven we will toil endlessly. We will not game the system, advance technologically, or so master productivity that we can stop striving.

And when we pass away, what will be left? We "must leave it to the man who will come after [us], and who knows whether he will be wise or a fool?" (2:19) Our legacy, our best efforts, will be in the hands of someone else, totally out of our control. The fruits of our labors, big or small, will be handed off, and we will likely be forgotten.

If we can't guarantee a lasting legacy through our work, what is the point?

This does not seem like very good news for us, but it is true. Ecclesiastes is diagnosing the self-centered sickness of our hearts and pointing us to something else. (I hope you're picking up a theme: all the bad news in Ecclesiastes points to something better.) So while this is not easy medicine to take, it is medicine nonetheless. Ecclesiastes is trying to get us to stop seeking identity, security, and fulfillment through work. The bad news has a healthful aim.

In the next study we'll look at the remedy Ecclesiastes offers us and how it directs us to approach and value work under the sun. To conclude this portion, though, pause to consider why we expect so much from our work, especially considering that all available evidence confirms what Ecclesiastes says: it is constant toil and striving after the wind if we are seeking identity and fulfillment from work.

Why do we look to work for appease the yearning for fulfillment in our hearts?

Personal Study 3

The Goodness of Work

Do you view work as a good thing, a bad thing, or a necessary evil? Why?

We tend to approach work in one of two ways. Either we need work to fulfill us (as we saw in the previous study) so we throw ourselves into it with fervor, even to the point of addiction. Or we use work to get us something else—comfort, ease, leisure, retirement—in which case we tend to give work the bare minimum to get us what we really want. So either work is our identity or our means to an end in seeking fulfillment.

Where else does the Bible describe work?

Read Genesis 1:28-31. What does Scripture teach about the place and purpose of work at creation?

Neither of these strategies are how the Bible intends for us to approach work, which is why both are guaranteed to leave us disappointed and burned out. The first expects too much from work and the second removes the value and dignity from work. Genesis 1 presents an entirely different understanding of work. God created the world, flawless and good, and the first thing He did was commission Adam to work.

How are the ways we think about work different from the goodness of work we see in creation?

Ecclesiastes

Our instinct is to think that's harsh; Adam had been around for five minutes and was already being put to work. But notice a few things. First, God didn't sit idly by and demand that Adam work. He gave responsibility for His precious, good creation to His image bearer. Adam was not given a task list but a purpose and a mission. He was to cultivate and care for God's world. Work is introduced into the Bible as a good thing, an aspect of honoring the Lord in His creation.

> **How did we get work so wrong? How did it go from good and God-honoring to idolatry and emptiness?**

> **Read Genesis 3:14-19.**

The curse which God put on the world is comprehensive and explains how everything went wrong: our relationship with God, with creation, with each other, and even with ourselves. Of course we're going to interact wrongly with work now by expecting the wrong things and seeking the wrong things and working for the wrong motives. This is the context Ecclesiastes steps into.

> *Everyone should eat and drink and take pleasure in all his toil—*
> *this is God's gift to man . . . there is nothing better than that a man*
> *should rejoice in his work, for that is his lot.*
> **ECCLESIASTES 3:13,22**

> **How does Ecclesiastes' teaching on work echo the goodness shown in Genesis 1? How does it reorient us toward the goodness of work as God designed?**

Reading Ecclesiastes, it's as if the author is waving Genesis 1 in front of our faces so we can't miss the point. Work is a gift. Enjoying work is a gift. The fruits of our labors (eating and drinking) are a gift. When it says all this is our "lot," it means our portion, the amount God has given us. And if God has given it, then it is enough to satisfy.

How do we enjoy work under the sun in a fallen world?
What does rejoicing in our work look like?

Even if we wholeheartedly accept this repeated reminder to take joy in our work because it is a gift from God, we still face the question of *How? How do we enjoy work that is vanity? How do we eat and drink and relish the fruits of our labors in a fallen world that is passing away?* It feels almost impossible sometimes.

First, we need to remember Genesis 1 and the purpose of work. It is intended to care for God's creation and reflect God's character and image. Most of us don't live in agrarian societies where we are planting and watering and pruning. But we can pursue good in our work, nonetheless. We can work with excellence. We can work with integrity. We can honor and uplift our coworkers. We can care for those in our sphere of influence and seek their well-being. By working this way, we are not seeking too much or too little from work but are exhibiting the image of God and being a Genesis 1 worker.

Second, we must heed Ecclesiastes 9:10:

> *Whatever your hand finds to do, do it with your might, for there is no work*
> *or thought or knowledge or wisdom in Sheol, to which you are going.*
> **ECCLESIASTES 9:10**

This isn't a command to burn ourselves out in all directions, but to live with purpose and intent. It reminds us that life is short, so we have a defined amount of time to give everything we've got to the lot God has provided for us. We have been given a life's work by God and we must do it with our might. When we seek to turn work into our identity, we have forgotten that God made it and gave it. When we seek to use work as a means to pleasure, we are not working toward God's aims nor do we tend to work with all our might.

Finally, we work and enjoy the fruits of our work with gratitude. When Ecclesiastes describes rejoicing and finding pleasure, it's in the context of being a recipient of God's good gifts. Work was never designed to deliver identity or as a mere means to leisure; it was for the reflection of God's image, the good of creation, and the flourishing of people. And we get to participate in that! So we praise the Lord for His generosity and we work with all our might for our days under the sun.

Wealth, Fame, and Power

Start

Use this section to get the conversation started.

In the previous session we looked at the place of work in our lives, both what we turn it into and what God intends for it to be. That is closely tied to this week's session on wealth, fame, and power. As we saw, we often use work as a means to something else rather than for the good God intends.

How is work connected to the pursuit of wealth, fame, and power?

How do we use our professions (or hobbies or passions) to gain wealth, fame, or power?

How are wealth, fame, and power connected?

Ecclesiastes doesn't explicitly say much about "fame," but it does talk about surpassing others. It also it describes people in positions of high status. These teachings relate to the topics of wealth, fame, and power. The three are inextricable because we pursue each one with the hopes of gaining the others. In pretty much every society in the world across history money is power, power brings fame, people can use their fame and power to get more money.

But this is not a mere study of sociology or economics. This is an exploration of the truths of Scripture, especially the light they shine on our hearts. So the pressing question of this session is—*Why do we so relentlessly pursue wealth, fame, and power?*

Watch

Take notes as you watch video session 4.

To access the teaching sessions,
use the instructions in the back
of your Bible study book.

Discuss

Use this section to guide your group discussion.

So far we have looked at the themes of wisdom and work in Ecclesiastes and now we are looking at the theme of wealth/fame/power. How do all these themes connect?

What common threads run through these themes?

When we read Ecclesiastes, it can be difficult to make sense of. It seems like the Solomon is jumping around from topic to topic. That's why this study is organized into themes, so you can see the coherence of the book. More importantly, though, is for you to see that the themes themselves fit together. It is not merely a series of disparate ideas, but a collection of interwoven realties from life.

Wisdom, work, wealth, fame, and power (and next session, justice) are tied together by the human heart. They are all things we turn to for significance, happiness, purpose, direction, fulfillment, and identity. We use one to gain others, and we keep going back to the well over and over again despite never being fully satisfied.

What does our pursuit of significance, happiness, purpose, direction, fulfillment, and identity through wisdom/work/wealth/fame/power say about our hearts?

Ecclesiastes is a diagnostic for our hearts. Living under the sun, we fall prey to sinful thinking that we can find ultimate meaning and happiness through things on earth. Most of these are good things (work, wisdom, justice, income) that we have turned into something more than God intended. This session focuses on three that are more difficult to label as "good."

Are wealth, fame, and power sinful, good, or neither? Explain. What positives and negatives do you associate with each?

Wealth, fame, and power are often associated with pride and ego. We think of how these can be taken to excess or abused. We might even harbor resentment against or scoff at wealthy, famous people in power.

If wealth, fame, and power are associated with pride, ego, excesses, and even abuse then why are they so tempting to us? Why do we still seek them out and want to at least be close to them?

On the other hand, if we're honest, we also would really like to try out being wealthy, famous, and powerful. Sure, it's not so good for those other people, but we would handle it better, right? And if we can't have them we at least want to see them, to be up close. All around us—on TV, social media, the news—we are tempted by the lures of wealth, fame, and power. It intrigues us and attracts us like moths to a light (and sometimes with the same results, as we'll see later).

It's not hard to see how we try to observe or be close to wealth, fame, and power. But how do we try to gain it? What do we do in our "normal" lives that is really grasping at these?

We work for money (wealth), and we often have our eye on the next position or promotion that might offer more. And with that promotion might come some additional authority or autonomy (power). And maybe we'll be recognized in the company for our contributions (fame). And with the recognition a bonus would be nice (wealth). We angle for these with almost every decision.

Ecclesiastes is not a book of judgment and condemnation. It offers warnings, but its main objective is to guide us toward godly wisdom. Ecclesiastes helps us order our priorities and weigh our values according to eternal truths. One of the ways it does this is by helping us see God's design for us and for our desires. It does the same with its teaching on wealth, fame, and power.

We must note that the book takes a more warning tone regarding these themes than the previous ones. That isn't because of inherent evil in wealth, fame, or power but because they deliver pleasure, and pleasure quickly becomes an idol. We are pleasure seekers, and that is a God-designed thing, and a good thing so long as we are seeking the right kinds of pleasures in the right places with the right expectations and gratitude.

What is the risk of pursuing wealth, fame, and power?

What does our desire for these things tell us about how God designed our hearts? What are we seeking to fulfill when we pursue them?

Close your time together with prayer.

Personal Study 1

Guided Reading

During the next week read the following verses to gain a deeper appreciation for what Ecclesiastes teaches about wealth, fame, and power

ECCLESIASTES 2:1-11

Solomon describes his vast efforts to find pleasure and meaning through building, cultivating, and collecting. He accumulated a mass of possessions, property, and treasure to the point where he surpassed all who came before him. He was the richest king in Israel's history, and maintained his wisdom. And in the end he describes it as "vanity and a striving after wind."

ECCLESIASTES 4:7-8

Ecclesiastes highlights the selfishness of constantly pursuing more and more wealth or status. It points out that people are not satisfied with "more," so they don't consider who they are collecting for. The object is gain, not the good of others.

ECCLESIASTES 4:13-16

These verses emphasize the value of wisdom and humility over power and wealth, especially when power and wealth move us away from a willingness to learn or heed advice. They also highlight the vanity of achieving power by pointing out that the one who climbs from humble and poor to rich and powerful will still be forgotten.

ECCLESIASTES 5:10-6:6

More than any other passage in Ecclesiastes, these verses emphasize the empti- ness of pursuing wealth. They move beyond the "vanity" of something that passes away into the emptiness of something that cannot satisfy, saying that the pursuit of wealth only leads to a desire for more wealth. It goes on to say that a person who is content in their work will be able to find rest while the wealthy simply accumulate reasons for anxiety and inability to enjoy life's good things. It points out the evil of both unfair business dealings that rob people of their earned income as well as the evil of death that robs people of their chance to enjoy what is earned.

Notes

Personal Study 2

The Lure of Influence

King Solomon was the wealthiest man of his day and likely the wealthiest king Israel ever had. He presided over Israel during a time of unprecedented peace and prosperity when the whole kingdom flourished. Solomon was known far and wide for his lavish home and treasury and for his brilliant mind, so kings and queens from around the world traveled to see him. He was filthy rich, a king over a kingdom at its apex, and respected by rulers from all over. So when Solomon speaks up about wealth, fame, and power we should take notice.

Read Ecclesiastes 2:1-11.

These words seem deeply personal. How does this affect your reading of them or how they land on you?

Let's examine how Solomon went about pursuing pleasures. There is a list of the things he did (building, collecting, storing, purchasing, etc.) but to sum up, "And whatever my eyes desired I did not keep from them. I kept my heart from no pleasure" (v. 10). He used every available means to collect wealth, power, and fame and all the pleasures they bring. "Power" and "fame" aren't mentioned specifically in the passage, but he was a king who could literally buy and sell people. He made deals with other rulers. He was known far and wide.

How does this description of Solomon's lifestyle and pursuits strike you? What stands out?

Of course, if you're doing this study it's unlikely you are a fabulously wealthy monarch with other monarchs clamoring for your attention. So our temptation would be to distance ourselves from these verses as inapplicable. But remember, Ecclesiastes goes after the heart, and the heart of Solomon is not different than the heart of a digital marketer, a mom, a student, a carpenter, or a banker. In his shoes we would've done the same thing, and in our current situation we do our best imitation.

How do we do the same thing Solomon did, at a "normal people" level?

Like Solomon, we do our best to "keep our hearts from no pleasure." As we mature, we learn that this must be done within reason, like an adult. And as Christians, we understand that there are moral boundaries on what kinds of pleasures we pursue. But we still go for it. More than tactile or sensual pleasures, we gravitate toward the things that seemingly deliver purpose and fulfillment. This is why Ecclesiastes emphasizes wealth, power, and fame rather than food, booze, and sex.

How do you seek fulfillment or pleasure from wealth, fame, or power?

Most of us don't think in terms like "wealth," "fame," and "power." Those are words that apply to, well, people like Solomon. But consider the following:

- *How often do you check your bank account?*
- *How often do you wish you owned something that is outside your budget?*
- *How often do you think it would be nice to get a raise?*

You don't have to be wealthy to yearn for wealth or love money. It is a matter of what your heart desires and what you are looking to for security and fulfillment.

- *Wouldn't it be nice to get more recognition at work?*
- *Doesn't it feel nice to be publicly acknowledged at church for your service?*
- *Do you know how many followers you have on social media?*
- *Do you check how many likes/shares/comments/replies you get on your posts? Do you get disappointed when the number is a bit low?*

You don't need to be famous to yearn for recognition and to be valued and praised. We love the praise of our fellow humans and find ways to position ourselves for it.

- *Do you hate when circumstances are out of your control?*
- *Do you try to position yourself for influence or authority in a group (friends, school PTO, church committee, etc.)?*
- *Wouldn't it be nice to be handed more responsibility or authority at work?*

Ecclesiastes

You don't need to be in a position of power to want power. Every time we try to gain control or influence or authority we are seeking power. It feels good to be looked up to and have people take you seriously.

Reconsider the previous question with these answers in mind. Where do you see your pursuit of wealth, fame, or power? What is the benefit of these pursuits?

Let's hear from Solomon again, what he had to say about the value and benefit of these pursuits.

I considered all that my hands had done and the toil I had expended in doing it, and behold, all was vanity and a striving after wind, and there was nothing to be gained under the sun.
ECCLESIASTES 2:11

He who loves money will not be satisfied with money, nor he who loves wealth with his income; this also is vanity.
ECCLESIASTES 5:10

Sweet is the sleep of a laborer, whether he eats little or much, but the full stomach of the rich will not let him sleep.
ECCLESIASTES 5:12

Why is Solomon so much more pointed about these pursuits than his previous warnings? How does the pursuit of wealth, fame, and power leave us feeling empty and anxious?

What we read from Solomon is his life's evidence that what Jesus would later say, "It is easier for a camel to go through the eye of a needle than for a rich man to enter the kingdom of heaven" (Matthew 19:24) is profoundly true. Not because money is bad but because our hearts are prone to worship wealth as our source of security, peace, and pleasure so that we don't rely on God. And the same goes for power and fame, influence and reputation. Solomon is coming for our idols to protect our hearts and turn us to God as our provider, the giver of purpose, and the source of our identity.

Personal Study 3

True Pleasure

Ever since I was a child I bucked against being told what not to do. Telling me not to do something was the quickest way to make me want to try it. I don't think I'm alone in this. On top of that, most of us aren't inspired toward lasting change by bad news. Bad news might scare us straight, but hope and promise keep us committed for the long haul. So rather than hammering on what not to do and what idols not to pursue, I want to offer some good news—a better picture from Scripture of what God wants for us.

Let's start at the very beginning. In Genesis 1 God created the world and He repeatedly called it good. The world was as it's supposed to be. Then God created humankind and verse 27 says "So God created man in his own image, in the image of God he created him; male and female he created them."

> **Take some time to reflect on what it means to be made in God's image. What comes to mind? What might this have to do with our inclination to pursue temporal things for fulfillment and identity?**

> **Take some time to consider a world that is truly good, a world in which our relationship with God is not broken. What would our deepest desires look like? What would we turn to for fulfillment and identity?**

We were made with deep desires, a profound purpose. We carry the very image of God. Yet sin twisted all that. It turned us away from what God intended for our fulfillment to seek God-sized desires in money, recognition, and power. Of course Solomon calls this all striving after the wind. How could a being like you or me be satisfied with so little?

> **What truths from Scripture can you think of that speak to God's design for the fulfillment of our desires and tell us of what He truly wants for us?**

Ecclesiastes

Ecclesiastes must be read as part of the whole of scripture. Read on its own, we are left with a clear picture of what doesn't work in life, where not to look for happiness or purpose or meaning. Read in the greater context of God's Word, it provides a contrast and a warning against our base, sinful nature under the sun. It points us to the good news by expounding on the bad news.

Solomon wrote of withholding pleasure from himself, and called it vanity. Psalm 16 paints a different picture. The entire psalm speaks of God's goodness in this life and for eternity, of His care and protection, and of His blessing. Here's how it concludes

> You make known to me the path of life; in your presence there is fullness
> of joy; at your right hand are pleasures forevermore.
> **PSALM 16:11**

What a contrast with the path Solomon took, exactly the contrast Solomon wants readers of Ecclesiastes to see. One pursuit of pleasure is striving after the wind, and another offers pleasures forevermore. This is God's intent, the design of Genesis 1.

What would it look like for you to pursue the pleasures that are offered in God's presence instead of the passing pleasures of this life?

What does this mean for us as we navigate life under the sun? Are we to eschew all pleasures and pursue an ascetic, pleasureless lifestyle? Ecclesiastes makes clear that is not the case. Such a pursuit would just be another version of seeking purpose and fulfillment through godless means.

What does it look like to find pleasure in this life without turning the pleasures into idols?

In Ecclesiastes 2:10 Solomon says he "found pleasure in all his toil"—the same refrain that runs through the whole book. This is followed immediately by saying all his pursuits of pleasure were vain, so what he is telling us is that there is pleasure to be found *but not ultimate pleasure*. There is enjoyment to be had, but not identity or fulfillment. We can appropriately approach the pleasures of this life with a smile and with gratitude to God. He is not condemning wealth or fame or power, he is putting them in their proper place.

Practically, these things should be results in life, not pursuits. In the last session we saw the God-honoring value of working with all our might. That kind of diligence always results in a meaningful life; working faithfully at what God has given you to do is always significant. For some it results in wealth or fame or power. But to pursue these things for their own sakes is to toy with temptation. This is difficult for us to accept because, well, we want to be rich and famous! But Solomon himself is our teacher and object lesson. He pursued these things, and it brought him low. It brought the whole kingdom of Israel low (see 2 Kings).

How can you resist the temptation to pursue more wealth, fame, and power/influence?

A constant theme in Ecclesiastes is lifting our eyes above the sun. That is what is happening here; we are being pulled away from the mesmerizing allure of earthly pleasures to look at the fulfillment offered in Jesus. Ecclesiastes never mentions Jesus. It never prophesies of Jesus. But it is about Jesus. How?

Because only in Christ can we find the fulfillment that was lost in the fall, that has been absent because of sin. Genesis 1 is a picture of perfect design leading to perfect happiness. That was lost because of sin and the righteous, holy judgment of God. But in Christ it is regained.

How does the gospel of Jesus Christ free us from a need for earthly pleasures to fulfill us?

Does Jesus take away our desire for earthly things? Not really. Rather, He reframes them and puts them in their proper place. When we have given ourselves to Jesus we no longer need earthly pleasures like wealth, fame, and power. Rather we can appreciate them without being governed by them. In the words of the early 20th century hymn, "Turn Your Eyes Upon Jesus":

> *Turn your eyes upon Jesus*
> *Look full, in his wonderful face*
> *And the things of earth will grow strangely dim*
> *In the light of his glory and grace*

WEEK 5

Justice

Start

Use this section to get the conversation started.

This session represents a shift of sorts. The last few sessions we have primarily looked at the human heart, our motivations and desires and pursuits. Now we are turning outward and looking more at the condition of the world under the sun. Thus far, we have touched on this, especially in terms of Genesis 3 and the effects of sin on the world, but now we are going to dig into how we interact with a broken world.

What responsibility does a Christian have to pursue what is right and just in the world? What difference does this make?

Working through this session, remember that we are still working within the reality of "vanity under the sun" and that "vanity" in Ecclesiastes doesn't mean "pointless" but rather that something will not last. This is important, because this session is largely about the desire for and the pursuit of justice and setting things right. Ecclesiastes calls this pursuit "vanity" too, and we must keep in mind that it is not saying the pursuit of justice is pointless.

Read Micah 6:8.

> *He has told you, O man, what is good;*
> *   and what does the LORD require of you*
> *but to do justice, and to love kindness,*
> *   and to walk humbly with your God?*
> MICAH 6:8

How does this verse help us understand the "vanity" aspect of justice in Ecclesiastes better?

Like the themes that have come before, Ecclesiastes offers a balance. The pursuit of justice is vain because it is not permanent. But it is good and right, the only way to make our way in a fallen world.

Watch

Take notes as you watch video session 5.

To access the teaching sessions, use the instructions in the back of your Bible study book.

Discuss

Use this section to guide your group discussion.

How does the phrase "life's not fair" ring true? Why or why not?

Consider the following statements.

- *How could that tragedy have happened to such a great person?*
- *How could such an awful person get away with that horrific deed?*
- *We lost him too soon.*

What do sentiments like these say about how we view the world and how we view what is fair or just?

Where do we get our sense of justice, our standard for right and wrong?

We all have a sense of justice, that people deserve certain rewards or consequences. And we live in a world where people don't always get what they deserve, for good or ill. Life isn't fair. And Ecclesiastes reinforces this with bluntness.

Read the following verses together.

> *In the place of justice, even there was wickedness, and in the place of righteousness, even there was wickedness.*
> **ECCLESIASTES 3:16**

> *I saw all the oppressions that are done under the sun. And behold, the tears of the oppressed, and they had no one to comfort them! On the side of their oppressors there was power.*
> **ECCLESIASTES 4:1**

> *If you see in a province the oppression of the poor and the violation of justice and righteousness, do not be amazed at the matter.*
> **ECCLESIASTES 5:8**

Like much of Ecclesiastes, it's easy to see statements like these as fatalistic. They sound like they are giving up and passively accepting the mess that injustice has made. They sound hopeless. To read them this way is to forget the context of Ecclesiastes: under the sun.

How does "under the sun" reframe these bleak statements about injustice?

In an "under the sun" reality, these are hopeless statements. If our present reality—distant from God and broken by sin—were the only possibility, injustice would absolutely rule. But the point of Ecclesiastes is to paint a bleak backdrop against which the brighter, truer, better reality of life "above the sun" can shine. The book is showing us how hopeless resisting injustice is apart from God and how the only hope for restoration is through Jesus Christ.

How does keeping our minds on "above the sun" reality help us navigate and resist injustice now?

Ecclesiastes goes further than simple "unfairness" in its dealing with injustice. It addresses the greatest evil, the greatest inequity: death. Death is the clearest mark that life under the sun is not the way God intended it to be. The existence of death is proof that something has gone terribly wrong. This is why we feel a deep ache or even become angry when we lose someone we love. Death is an injustice we cannot resist or correct.

How does the ubiquity of death lift our eyes above the sun? Where does it force us to look for hope?

Death is literally the end of ourselves, so when we face it we are confronted with the reality that we can do nothing about it. In the face of any other injustice, we can deceive ourselves into thinking we have the solution. In the face of death, we are brought face to face with the truth that we need someone infinitely greater to solve the problem. So as you study these passages from Ecclesiastes, look for the places where Christ is the only solution. Ecclesiastes won't say this explicitly, but it erases all the other options.

Close your time together with prayer.

Ecclesiastes

Personal Study 1
Guided Reading

During the next week read the following sections of Ecclesiastes to gain a greater appreciation for what it teaches about justice.

ECCLESIASTES 2:21

It is "a great evil" that people work hard and toil, only for the fruits of their labors to be enjoyed by others who did not work for it.

ECCLESIASTES 3:16-22

The world is upside down and backwards in many ways. Where there should be righteousness and goodness there is wickedness. We can find some comfort in the fact that God is testing and God will judge; He is not absent. Under the sun, all man's efforts don't functionally make us better than any living thing because we all pass away. (This does not diminish the value of being an image bearer of God, but rather highlights that under the sun even that magnificent reality doesn't keep us from death.)

ECCLESIASTES 4:1-16

This passage highlights how bad things can get under the sun. Power is on the side of the oppressors and power is used to oppress. It creates such bleak realities that sometimes it seems like those who have passed away or have never been born are better off than the living. It goes on to point out solutions that will not resolve these inequities or this pain: wealth, comfort, toil. It then highlights the value of and need for friendship in this broken world and concludes by pointing out that even rulers are forgotten and their leadership is vanity.

ECCLESIASTES 5:8-9

These two verses offer some balance. Do not be surprised when you see the poor being oppressed by the rich and powerful, but it is still better to have a ruler that works for the good of the people than to tear down power altogether.

ECCLESIASTES 6:6-12

These verses point out that no matter how a person lives, he achieves the same end, death. There is no advantage to the wise or the righteous. It then offers a realistic balance to remind us that it is still better to have the sight of wisdom than to give ourselves over to our appetites. The passage concludes with the brooding question, "Who knows what is good?" This is a pressing question under the sun, and one that cannot be answered apart from reality with God.

ECCLESIASTES 8:1-13

This passage offers clarity on the value of wisdom and obedience in the face of injustice and evil. While some of Ecclesiastes could (wrongly) be interpreted as saying morality and righteousness come to nothing, these verses emphasize the importance of obedience to the law, standing for good, and pursuing wisdom, even in the face of death and evil. It concludes with a vital reminder that we need to fear God to be able to find hope and have solid footing. Because God will set things right and will judge justly in His timing.

ECCLESIASTES 9:1-6

These verses expound upon the reality that death is "an evil that is done under the sun," reflecting the curse of Genesis 3 and how death is our consequence for sin. They make clear that it is evil for its very existence and because it treats everyone the same regardless of how good their lives are. Finally, it pointedly declares the value of life by saying "a living dog is better than a dead lion," so we should live our lives to the fullest.

ECCLESIASTES 9:11-12

This passage provides a concluding statement about the unfairness and unpredictability of death as the great evil and injustice.

Personal Study 2

The Problem of Injustice

Few things are more inspiring and truly wholesome than stories of justice triumphing—William Wilberforce working tirelessly to outlaw the slave trade in England, the women's suffrage movement gaining women the right to vote, the Civil Rights movement, from sit-ins to marches to bus boycotts, moving the country to pass the Civil Rights Act. Even just a school yard bully being put in his place by another brave child is inspiring. We love to see things set right and injustice thrown down.

Why do stories like these move us so much and resonate so deeply?

The desire for justice is a God-given desire, and more than that it is God-reflecting. It's a longing to see the world returned to the goodness of Genesis 1 and creation reflect God's order and intent. Whether or not a person believes in Jesus or professes to be a Christian, the yearning for justice is a reflection of God's image in us.

Think through history. How have the great stories of justice ended? Where has society gone after those stories ended?

Read Ecclesiastes 3:16-22 and 4:1-16.

Ecclesiastes reminds us of a hard reality, though. Our desire for justice, no matter how good, does not govern life under the sun. Chapters 3 and 4 especially describe the upside down, backward reality of life under the sun. There is evil where there should be righteousness. There is injustice where there should be justice. Power is with the oppressors. All our best efforts to set things right will not ultimately fix things.

What does Ecclesiastes teach about ways we try to respond to injustice?

Think of the examples I gave earlier—Wilberforce, the suffrage movement, Civil Rights, school yard bullies. Each is a story of great achievement, of justice winning the day. But that's the thing, justice wins days not eternity. Chattel slavery was eradicated, but racism was not. Women gained the vote, but sexism was not eliminated. The Civil Rights movement erased legal segregation, but de facto segregation and racial inequality exists to this day. And for every schoolyard bully that gets knocked down another one shows up to steal lunch money and stick kids in garbage cans. All the best efforts of humanity did good, but they were vain. They were not enough to bring about permanent redemption and justice.

When you read that justice is "vanity" how does that strike you?
Where do you see it to be true in the world around you?

How would you define "injustice"?

One thing we notice in Ecclesiastes is that "injustice" is not primarily a legal or criminal idea. It is not described in terms of the law, prosecution, or restitution. Criminality falls into the category of injustice, but injustice is so much more. It is described in terms of unrighteousness and of evil. Injustice is doing things outside of the way God intended, in a way that leads to demeaning or diminishing someone else. Injustice is sin committed by a person or a group that has a victim or victims.

What are examples of injustice that fall outside the areas of legality
or criminality?

This sweeping definition of injustice puts things in much starker reality for us. It is the way of life under the sun, the direct outworking of Genesis 3. It is the outworking of our sinful hearts toward others seeking to subjugate or oppress, and the more earthly power we gain the more ability we have to perpetrate injustice. It is the natural way of human interactions, individually and collectively the world over; one side is looking to gain an advantage or benefit from the other side. It is the way of life under the sun: entropy, decay, decline, a trend toward conflict and chaos. Especially the end of life.

Read Ecclesiastes 9:1-6 and 11-12.

How should the universal nature of death cause us to focus on the reality above the sun?

Death is universal in its sweep. It is an event that is outside of what God intended that victimizes both the ones taken and the ones left behind. No matter how well we live, death comes for us all. It cares not whether a person is wise, foolish, righteous, evil, poor, or rich. While death is equitable—it comes for us all—it is unfair in its distribution and evil in its existence.

What does irresolvable injustice do to your spirit and your outlook on life?

If human efforts cannot solve injustice under the sun, what is our way forward? How do we live? What is our hope?

This pervasive, oppressive reality of unsolvable injustice is what leaves us with the aching sensation of frustration and "this isn't right." It can leave us manic in our efforts to fix it, exhausting ourselves and working to a frenzy. It can leave us cynical, tapped out, and detached as we watch the world burn. Or it can move us to faithfulness to God and toward his creation. This is what we will look at in the next session.

What does faithfulness look like in a world of overwhelming injustice we cannot fix?

Personal Study 3

Pursuing Justice

Ecclesiastes is not a book of instructions. Rarely in its twelve chapters do you find clear, practical commands or directions on how to live. Instead, it paints pictures of how things are, and we can see how things ought to be in the white spaces of those pictures. It paints a picture of how pervasive injustice is and the limitations we have to correct it. In so doing it doesn't offer us a code of conduct but rather an outline of what a justice-loving life can look like.

What have you learned about where not to look for hope in solving injustice? What does this suggest as the place to look?

As we've seen, Ecclesiastes makes clear that all our human efforts, no matter how well-intentioned, cannot wholly reverse injustice. But it is not saying to give up.

Read Ecclesiastes 8:1-13.

What in these verses offers some clear direction and hope?

These verses emphasize three things: lawfulness, wisdom, and fear of the Lord.

Lawfulness can be understood as obedience. Are we following the commands of our rulers? This is not a blind obedience, as we can see from verse 2 where it mentions the Lord's oath to the king. Obviously, we are no longer under the rule of a king anointed by God, so this means that we are called to obey so long as the law of the land is not opposed to Christianity. As Christians, it is our duty and responsibility to obey our government.

How does lawfulness contribute to justice?

Lawfulness contributes to a just society by encouraging peaceable interactions between citizens and government. The more people live lawfully, the more society is mutually beneficial rather than mutually harmful. It is a neighborly, humble, and God-honoring way to live.

The second thing emphasized in these verses is wisdom. Now, we already studied the vanity of wisdom, so you may raise an eyebrow at this. But remember that wisdom offers strength, gives sight, and inclines our hearts away from foolishness. Chapter 8 doesn't mention wisdom explicitly, but it depicts it when it says in verse 6 "there is a time and a way for everything" and when verse 9 refers to applying one's heart to all that happens under the sun. These are pictures of navigating and weighing life wisely, applying the reality of God to life under the sun.

How does wisdom contribute to justice?

Verse 6 is striking as we consider how to apply wisdom to unsolvable injustice: "For there is a time and a way for everything, although man's trouble lies heavy on him." This isn't a promise of resolution, but of progress, of making it. While that doesn't sound idealistic or victorious, it is profound. The Lord has a way forward for us, and wisdom is how we discern and follow it. No, it will not remove all the trouble, but it will take us forward in faithfulness.

The third and final thing emphasized in these verses is the fear of the Lord. Verses 12-13 offer a promise about the reward for fearing the Lord and the cost for refusing to do so. It is as clear as any in Ecclesiastes, about what direction our hearts should be facing even, especially, in the face of injustice. The Lord is on the side of those who fear Him, and He will not lose or fail. This promise is in our faces because God knows that the burden of facing injustice daily rattles our faith and makes us wonder how to proceed. So He tells us how.

What does fearing the Lord in the midst of injustice look like?

Verse 11 helps us see what fearing the Lord in the face of injustice means. It says, "the sentence against an evil deed is not executed speedily"and that sets up the promise we just looked at. How striking that the precursor to a certain promise is a statement that we must wait on the Lord! Fearing the Lord means believing verses

12-13 while we live in the reality of verse 11. We know God will do justice while we wait (sometimes for what feels like a painfully long time) for Him to act. Waiting in faith is fearing the Lord because it is living as if God is real and what He says is undeniably true.

How does fearing the Lord lay a foundation for us as we pursue justice?

If God is real and His word is undeniably true, what else has He said that we ought to consider as we navigate this unjust, broken life under the sun? The answer is that He has said so much. The Bible is deep and rich with counsel, commands, promises, wisdom, stories, and teaching to show us God's way. But let's close this session by considering two verses.

> *He has told you, O man, what is good; and what does the LORD require of you*
> *but to do justice, and to love kindness, and to walk humbly with your God?*
> **MICAH 6:8**

In the midst of injustice we are to do justice. We are to be the embodiment of God's purposes for the world, pushing back the darkness. We are to love mercy, so our attempts at justice will dignify and comfort the weak and vulnerable and they will refuse to be combative and heavy-handed against our foes. And we must walk humbly with our God. To walk with God means to be close to Him daily, following Him faithfully. And we do this humbly. There is no room for hubris or arrogance as we seek to uphold justice and care for the victimized.

> *You shall love your neighbor as yourself.*
> **MARK 12:31**

Paul says in Galatians that the whole law is fulfilled by obeying this verse. To love our neighbor as ourselves is not merely to have warm feelings, but to seek his or her best. It means to seek their well-being, their thriving, their dignity. Just the same way we instinctively do for ourselves. In short, to love our neighbor as ourselves is to seek justice for our neighbor. We cannot eradicate injustice. But we can do justice, love mercy, walk humbly with God, and love our neighbors. It may not turn society right side up, but it will invite people into a better reality, the one we have confidence in because we fear the Lord. And we know that there will be a day when God will fully eradicate injustice (Revelation 21:4). Until that day we live lawfully, pursue God's wisdom, and fear the God who will make all things new through His Son.

Number Your Days

Start

Use this section to get the conversation started.

Death is an undeniable reality, and death is an undeniable evil. Ecclesiastes makes both of these realities abundantly clear. Last session we saw that death is a great evil, a great injustice. It is also something we can do nothing about and all of us must face.

Why is it so difficult for us to discuss death?

Why do we never grow more at ease with death despite the fact that it is undeniable and unavoidable?

Death is one of the primary themes of Ecclesiastes. Why is this so? Because death defines life. It is quite literally the boundary of our lives. We do all we can to avoid the concept of death: age-defying treatments, euphemistic language, outsourcing of hospice and end-of-life care so people die in seclusion instead of in homes. We are essentially plugging our ears and closing our eyes and yelling "la la la I can't hear you!"

But none of this avoids the reality of death. It is around us all the time, whether we want to acknowledge it or not. It is coming for us all (9:3). But is this a threat, a warning, or an opportunity? Ecclesiastes offers much wisdom on how to think about it, but you must be willing to wade into dark waters and face some realities we Westerners find quite uncomfortable.

Does discussing death push you more toward depression or toward motivation to live well? Does it diminish your life or fuel your life? Why?

Watch

Take notes as you watch video session 6.

To access the teaching sessions,
use the instructions in the back
of your Bible study book.

Discuss

Use this section to guide your group discussion.

In the brilliant 1991 movie, *What About Bob?*, uber neurotic and unstable Bob Wiley befriends the family of his psychologist, the perfectly smug and superior Leo Marvin. Leo has a middle school aged son named Siggy (after Sigmund Freud, of course), a brooding boy who wears all black and has a fixation with death. At one point in the movie middle-aged Bob and Siggy have this conversation:

> Siggy: *Bob, are you afraid of death?*
>
> Bob: *Yeah.*
>
> Siggy: *Me too, but there's no way out of it. You're going to die. I'm going to die. It's going to happen, and what difference does it make if it's tomorrow or eighty years . . . much sooner in your case. Do you know how fast time goes? I was six, like, yesterday.*
>
> Bob: *Me too.*
>
> Siggy: *I'm going to die. You are going to die. What else is there to be afraid of?*

Setting aside the seeming unhealth of a middle schooler fixated on death, what does Siggy get right? What is helpful about his words?

Dark humor helps ease the pain of a discussion about death. And it's at least a little easier to stomach the statement "You're going to die. I am going to die" when it comes packaged in a ninety minute movie. Don't miss the point, though. Siggy might be in a bad frame of mind, but he is not wrong. Death is a certainty, death is inescapable, and that means death is something we cannot afford to ignore.

What is the cost or consequence of avoiding the reality of death?

Ecclesiastes is laced with death. You cannot read any portion and not come in contact with the reality of your mortality. We started this study by looking at the reality that all is vanity under the sun. Well, "vanity" and "under the sun" is an introduction to mortality. It addresses the temporal nature of existence. Vanity, the concept that defines every theme we've discussed thus far, is defined by things coming to an end and by the people pursuing those things coming to an end. We cannot avoid mortality in Ecclesiastes. Nor should we want to.

How does death shape life? How should it shape life?

Ecclesiastes is wisdom literature. It is a revelation of God's wisdom to us, and it is clear that God wants us to be willing and able to navigate the "under the sun" reality of death. He wants us to gaze on the darkness so that the light shines brighter. Because while death is the stop button on life under the sun, it is not the final reality for Christians.

What do you think God wants us to see about death from Ecclesiastes? What wisdom does He want us to gain for navigating life?

Ecclesiastes presents death as the end, but that is from the perspective of life under the sun. How should Christians think about death?

The next three sessions will make a shift in our study of Ecclesiastes. We started with context, then we walked through four themes of navigating life that Ecclesiastes emphasizes (wisdom, work, wealth/fame/power, justice). Now we are shifting context from "under the sun" to "above the sun." Or rather, we are introducing "above the sun" perspectives into our "under the sun" life. All of Ecclesiastes intends to lift our eyes above the sun, to show us our need for reality with God. These final sessions will make that explicit, an invitation above the sun.

How would a shift from an "under the sun" perspective and context to an "above the sun" one mean for our thinking about death?

Close the session with prayer.

Personal Study 1

Guided Reading

During the next week read the following verses to gain a deeper appreciation for what Ecclesiastes teaches about the finite nature of life.

ECCLESIASTES 3:1-8

These verses give an invaluable context and framework for Ecclesiastes, especially a consideration of mortality and life under the sun. They begin by saying that everything "under heaven" has a season, meaning that in this life everything will have a beginning and an end. Everything has a lifespan, as verse 2 clearly states, "a time to be born, and a time to die." These verses are not saying that everything is good in its season, but rather that under the sun everything has a season. It is a depiction of life's complexities, tensions, and difficulties. Neither is this offering up a "que sera, sera, whatever will be will be" shrug as if we are to approach life passively. Rather, it is explaining the vanity of all things; they will all begin and they will all end, for good or ill. This is the reality of life and mortality we must navigate under the sun.

ECCLESIASTES 3:16-22

A stark look at mortality, these verses present in-your-face reality. All living things face the same end, there is no advantage for man over beast or for one class of human over another. The verses also ponder the mystery of death and the afterlife, "Who knows whether the spirit of man goes upward and the spirit of the beast goes down into the earth?" They conclude by regrounding us in an appreciation of life. Rather than being swept away in the darkness and mystery of death, it is better that we should rejoice in our work, for that is what God has provided us.

ECCLESIASTES 6:10-12

These verses are somewhat cryptic (as is a fair portion of Ecclesiastes). They are asking questions that ponder the value of life, and the value of investing in life. What is the payoff? They come on the heels of a passage that depicts the fruitlessness of seeking satisfaction and fulfillment through the pleasures of this life, so it is a natural question to raise: how do we live this life well, and what is its worth?

ECCLESIASTES 9:1-6

These verses emphasize the ubiquity of death. It happens to the righteous and the wicked, the wise and the foolish, the law keeper and the lawbreaker. In the end we are all the same. But the verse is not passive because it calls this an evil; it is wrong that death treats every living person the same. The passage ends by highlighting the value of life. It isn't a fiery inspirational verse but rather a blunt comparison: it's better to be a living dog (not very dignified) than a dead lion (dignified, but dead). All the meaningful things of life are left behind in death.

Notes

A Word of Context about Reading Ecclesiastes

I picked these passages for this session because they directly address death and the value of life. However, Ecclesiastes addresses death on every page. Life under the sun is defined by mortality—the sun setting on our days. Vanity is defined by mortality—things coming to an end. Life above the sun is defined by immortality—eternal life with God. So these realities and themes are inescapable throughout the book.

Personal Study 2

The End of Your Days

Read Ecclesiastes 3:1-8.

When Ecclesiastes 3 says there is a season for everything, how are we to understand that?

The beginning of Ecclesiastes 3 might be the best known passage in the book. It's not unusual for this passage to be used as a sort of explanation or comfort when life is hard. "I know you're going through some hard times, but your time to laugh will come." While this isn't wrong in spirit, it does misunderstand the passage. These verses are not saying for every time of weeping there will be a time of joy to balance it out.

They are more descriptive than they are a promise. They depict tension and complexity and even a hint of confusion. They paint a picture of a life that demands wisdom to be able to navigate it well. These verses are a statement of how the world is, not of how it ought to be, because they depict reality shaped by the curse of Genesis 3.

How do you see the curse of Genesis 3 reflected in Ecclesiastes 3:1-8?

God did not create the world with death and mourning and pain and fighting and loss. But sin and its consequences brought those to pass, and these verses describe that reality. We live in it, and we cannot change it, so we must come to terms with it. That's right, we must come to terms with the reality of death. But we do not have to like it or make peace with it.

How do we hold this tension between accepting the reality of death and refusing to make peace with it?

Ecclesiastes 9 (among other passages) makes clear that death "is an evil in all that is done under the sun" (v. 3). It is a thief and a victimizer. It is unjust, as we saw last session, because it reflects the broken state of the world and takes no consideration of worth or quality of life. When you read of someone's "untimely death" your first thought should be that no death is timely. When you hear of a young person who was "gone too soon" it is absolutely true, and it's just as true of your grandparents. Death is always an enemy, always an evil.

There are two ways we can try to come to terms with death under the sun, and only one of them works. The first is to rationalize death. We do this by rating some lives as more valuable than others based on accomplishment or age or affection toward them. We try to explain away the evil of death. Even in the case of criminals executed for crimes death is an evil because, whether you believe in the death penalty or not, death is still a thing that should not be. At best, and this is a stretch, death could be called a necessary evil, something that brought about a greater good. Rationalizing death may offer some temporary peace on occasion, but as a whole it doesn't work. It is not comprehensive. And it in no way solves the evil of death. The best it can do is try to outweigh some deaths with some perceived benefit.

Do you ever find yourself trying to rationalize death? If so, how?

Has rationalizing death brought you lasting peace and comfort?

The second way we can come to terms with death is by following the path of Jesus. This is what Ecclesiastes wants us to see, and the reason it is so blunt about death but offers no definitive comforts.

Read John 11:35, 1 Corinthians 15:26, and Revelation 20:14. How do these passages speak about death? What do they teach us about how we should view death as Christians?

Jesus wept over the death of his friend, Lazarus. He wept despite knowing He was about to raise Lazarus from the dead (John 11:35). Why did He weep? Not hopelessness or empty grief. He wept out of anger at the cost of death, the evil of death. He wept for the loss that death brings.

Paul described death as "the last enemy to be destroyed" (1 Corinthians 15:26). It puts verbiage to that feeling you have in your gut, that hatred toward death. It is the enemy. And what is more, it will be destroyed by Jesus.

The last book of the Bible promises the damnation of death (Revelation 20:14). Death will burn when Jesus returns; it will be thrown into the lake of fire. This is the extent to which death is evil and an enemy.

What comfort and hope do these verses give you?

Death is the final word under the sun, but death is not the final word. It hurts. It robs. It takes. It leaves scars on all of us and comes for us all. But it has already lost. Those verses promise us that the death of death is sure through Jesus Christ. And they invite us into reality and life above the sun.

How do we access and hold fast to "above the sun" reality while we live under the sun?

We live under the sun and see dimly what is above. But Jesus brought that eternal, glorious reality to earth in the incarnation. He ushered in a means to life above the sun. And He set the example for how to live under the sun in the face of death. He wept at the evil of death, He preached eternal life, He laid down his life for all who would believe, and He rose from the grave in victory over death. Jesus lived life under the sun to the fullest.

Personal Study 3

Better Alive than Dead

Read Ecclesiastes 9:4.

> *But he who is joined with all the living has hope,*
> *for a living dog is better than a dead lion.*
> **ECCLESIASTES 9:4**

Restate this verse in your own words. What is Solomon getting at here?

My grandfather was exceptional at the backhanded compliment. His praise for a good meal was something like *Could've been worse. Not bad* was his equivalent of *Way to go, I'm so proud of you!* You had to learn how to interpret these muted praises to understand their full import. Ecclesiastes 9:4 reads a little like a compliment from my granddad. Most people wouldn't be thrilled at being called "a living dog"; it's not flattering. But it's undeniable that being one is better than being a dead lion, who was once majestic and glorious but is now just gone.

After all our reflections on the evils of death, a statement like this is both jarring and exceptionally helpful. It's jarring because it's so pragmatic, and it's helpful because it pulls us out of existential, mortal dread and into the mindset of actually living. And that is the pressing question for us: how do we live in light of death?

As we saw, "there is a time for everything under heaven" is a description of our present state of reality, and we must live in it. The only way to live a meaningful, fruitful life under the sun is to deal in reality and respond with godly wisdom. Christians should be the most realistic people on earth, neither denying nor paralyzed by mortality.

What does it look like to live a full, meaningful life in light of mortality?

When you consider the comparison of being a living dog vs. a dead lion, it offers clarity. It crystallizes the value of life, even a simple life or a struggling life.

Read Ecclesiastes 9:5.

For the living know that they will die, but the dead know nothing, and they have no more reward, for the memory of them is forgotten.
ECCLESIASTES 9:5

How does Ecclesiastes 9:5 clarify our priorities in life?

Knowing we will die offers opportunity and motivation; it offers a chance at the reward of a life well-lived even if we never achieve the status of "lion." If we live seeking "lion" status—seeking fame, wealth, power, or great achievements—we might succeed. But to what end? The lion is forgotten in death. The reward was received and is gone too. In death, the lion is equal to every other creature.

At first, this reality seems enervating and discouraging. What is the point of living well if it will all just be forgotten anyhow? The point is that living well makes a difference during our time under the sun. Living in light of death means maximizing whatever days we have in life to bring "above the sun" reality to bear here and now.

We studied wisdom, work, wealth/fame/power, and justice. How does living in light of death shape how we pursue these things?

Our pursuit of wisdom will not reverse the foolishness in the world, but it will bring light and offer truth to others. It will guide our lives in fear of the Lord.

Our work will not offer identity or ultimate satisfaction, but we can do good through it. We can earn a wage with which we are generous and care well for others. We can accomplish meaningful tasks that improve our small part of the world. We can reflect the image of God in our diligence, creativity, and leadership.

Our notoriety, wealth, and power will not fill up our souls, but to whatever extent we have them they provide opportunities to do good. Fame, in whatever circle we have it, gives us a public voice for righteousness and good and justice. Wealth is a gift from God to be invested back into His work through the church and to meet needs. Power and authority are a profound opportunity to redirect circumstances, rules, policies, and even laws for the good of people. Power can be abused for our benefit or used as Christ used His, to lift up those who could never lift themselves. Our yearning for justice will not make the world a good place, but it can make our small neighborhood of the world a better place. We cannot right all the wrongs, but we can use our days to defend the weak and push back the darkness of injustice.

How does living in light of death clarify our expectations in this life?

I said earlier that Christians should be the most realistic people on earth, and living in light of death helps us with that too. It puts boundaries on our expectations. When we realize that all is vanity because of death, our expectations fall into line. We see our own limitations and the limitations of others more clearly. This realization does two things. First, it reduces the unreasonable burden of expectations we put on each other. Second, it moves all those massive hopes and expectations on to God, the only one who can truly bear them.

Death is evil. It is injustice. It is the enemy. So how does living in light of death point us to hope?

Ecclesiastes insists that we number our days. But it is not intended to dampen our outlook. It intends to shift our outlook from seeking hope, identity, and fulfillment under the sun to finding them above the sun. Living in light of death steals all joy and all purpose from our lives under the sun. Everything becomes "What's the point?" But living life in light of death is the backdrop of deepest joy and total fulfillment if our eyes are above the sun. This life truly matters if we see it as a runway to eternal life with Christ. Death is not the inescapable monster if we remember that Christ already defeated it.

Enjoy the Life God has Given You

Start

Use this section to get the conversation started.

How have the last couple sessions left you feeling? Are you wondering if/where the joy is to be found in Ecclesiastes?

After a session on the depths of injustice and then one on death, it's wonderful to turn our attention to something joyful. Ecclesiastes is not intended to depress us or be dark, and this session will focus on one of the clearest ways that is true.

Last session we looked at what it means to live our life well in light of the reality of mortality. Well, the theme of this session actually helps clarify that. It shows us where joy can be found under the sun.

Read the following verses to set the tone for this session.

> Go, eat your bread with joy, and drink your wine with a merry heart, for God has already approved what you do. Let your garments be always white. Let not oil be lacking on your head. Enjoy life with the wife whom you love, all the days of your vain life that he has given you under the sun, because that is your portion in life and in your toil at which you toil under the sun. Whatever your hand finds to do, do it with your might.
> **ECCLESIASTES 9:7-10**

Throughout Ecclesiastes we find this theme; we can't miss it. This is our portion. This is from God. He looks on His people with approval. So we can get to it.

What are some places and things you find joy in?

If all is vanity under the sun why and how do we enjoy the good things of life with gladness?

Watch

Take notes as you watch video session 7.

To access the teaching sessions,
use the instructions in the back
of your Bible study book.

Discuss

Use this section to guide your group discussion.

In the Bible repetition often communicates emphasis. All the themes we've looked at so far were repeated throughout Ecclesiastes, telling us they were something of which we should take note. This final theme is repeated several times throughout the book, and it strikes a different tone than the others. Instead of a warning or corrective tone, it is clearly there to encourage us.

> **Read Ecclesiastes 5:18-19, which strikes a different tone than much of what we've read so far.**

> > *Behold, what I have seen to be good and fitting is to eat and drink and find enjoyment in all the toil with which one toils under the sun the few days of his life that God has given him, for this is his lot. Everyone also to whom God has given wealth and possessions and power to enjoy them, and to accept his lot and rejoice in his toil—this is the gift of God.*
> > **ECCLESIASTES 5:18-19**

Ecclesiastes has a bright refrain to break the minor key of the book. Other passages phrase it differently, but the theme is the same. It is telling us to enjoy ourselves, to take pleasure in the good things of life.

> **While this sounds really nice, especially after the last couple sessions, how is "eat, drink, and enjoy yourself" in a world where all is vanity, not just fiddling while Rome burns or dining as the Titanic sinks?**

These verses almost sounds dissonant, out of place, after all we've studied about vanity and death and the brokenness of the world. Ecclesiastes points to the vanity then says, "so, go eat, drink, and find joy." At first, this might sounds a lot like the nihilistic attitude of "eat, drink, and be merry, for tomorrow we die."

But there is a key element to this command that separates it from this sort of "life is terrible and means nothing, so have fun while you've got the chance" attitude. Ecclesiastes repeatedly tells us that to find joy, to enjoy good things is our lot, something given by God. We are not finding pleasure to numb the pain or fill up the void, we are enjoying gifts from God.

**How do we keep our pursuit of enjoyment from becoming idolatry?
How do we avoid the pitfalls we've seen previously of using temporal
things in an attempt to give us purpose or identity?**

How do we receive gifts? With gratitude. What is the best way to show our gratitude? First to express it then to use the gift exactly as it is intended. To enjoy God's good gifts with relish, to deeply appreciate them and take pleasure in them, honors Him. And gratitude to the giver keeps the pleasure from becoming an idol. We can't be thankful to God and worship the gifts He gives us at the same time.

**How does this theme from Ecclesiastes adjust your view of God?
What does it show you about His character?**

Ecclesiastes has made abundantly clear that life under the sun is full of brokenness and disappointment. It's made clear that we cannot put our hopes in temporal things. It's made clear that we cannot fix the brokenness ourselves. And it has made clear that what we need is a reality that is above the sun, not defined by death and vanity.

How does this theme point to reality with God above the sun?

This command to find joy in God's good gifts, to thrive in our work, might seem like it's taking our eyes off of the eternal promise of life with God. But it's actually doing the opposite. Every pleasure God gives under the sun is like an appetizer of what is to come. Every delicious bite of food, every laugh we share with friends, every good day of work is a hint of the joy and fulfillment that is to come in eternity.

**What kind of freedom does this command to enjoy God's gifts give you?
How does it reorient your perspective and life?**

We need this command. Under the sun we tend to either dive into idolatry or to flee pleasurable things out of suspicion. In both cases we are misusing God's creation and good gifts. We need permission to enjoy what he has given us and we need a reminder that we're still under the sun. So these good gifts are not our ultimate satisfaction, but they are daily mercies God has for us so that we find happiness and pleasure under the sun, even in the middle of a messed up world.

Close the session with prayer.

Personal Study 1

Guided Reading

During the next week read the following verses to gain a deeper appreciation for what Ecclesiastes teaches about enjoyment.

ECCLESIASTES 3:1-8

These verses tell us that there is a time for everything under the sun. The previous session highlighted that there is a time for hard, painful things. This session highlights that there is a time for joyful things too: healing, laughter, dancing, embracing, love, peace. God's creative fingerprints are all over this world, and it is full of good gifts He has given us. The world is broken, they tell us, but it is not all bad.

ECCLESIASTES 3:9-15

These verses make clear that it is God's design for man to find joy and do good, and that there is nothing better under the sun. It underpins this statement by declaring that what God does lasts forever, so His design can be entirely trusted. The final sentence says that God seeks what has been driven away, meaning He intends to restore what was lost at the fall.

ECCLESIASTES 5:18-20

This passage is a clear command to take joy in the pleasures of life. It makes clear they are from God, our "lot." It concludes by pointing out that this kind of joy and gratitude will outweigh the burdens and pains of life under the sun.

ECCLESIASTES 7:14

This verse is especially important because of the clarity with which it declares that God is over both our good days and our bad ones, He provides the days of pleasure and the days of adversity.

ECCLESIASTES 8:15

This verse is as clear and concise a commendation of joy and pleasure as you will find. It is a sort of defiance of pain and sadness that comes with life under the sun.

ECCLESIASTES 9:7-10

This passage is the clearest and most comprehensive command in Ecclesiastes when it comes to enjoyment and gratitude. It paints a picture of thriving, pleasure, health, and vigor all because God provides and gives. It also juxtaposes the opportunity to give our all in this life with the emptiness of death.

ECCLESIASTES 11:8-10

A reminder that we should live life with vigor and purpose and enjoyment because the dark days, referring to death, are many. It is also a reminder to rejoice in youth rather than squandering it but not to dwell on the pain or trouble that will inevitably come with age.

Notes

Personal Study 2

Nothing Better

In the beginning God created the heavens and the earth . . .
and God saw that it was good.
GENESIS 1:1,10

How does the story of creation, specifically the goodness of creation, help us understand these commands from Ecclesiastes to enjoy God's good gifts?

When God made the world, He made it good. And not any kind of good you or I are familiar with. God made the world flawless, everything worked exactly as it was supposed to. Everything worked in harmony. Nothing decayed. If all is vain under the sun now, at creation nothing was. God walked with man, and creation thrived as God designed it to.

How does the story of the fall of man in Genesis 3 and God's curse on the earth reframe our expectations for pleasure?

In Genesis 3 human sin changed all that. Adam and Eve rebelled against God, seeking to be their own gods. God's holy and just response was to utter a curse that touched every aspect of creation and life. From that point forward life under the sun became vanity. Nothing works the way it is supposed to. Decay and death became inevitable. Under the sun became a universal context because the relationship between humankind, creation, and God was broken. This is where we live now, as Ecclesiastes clearly depicts.

So when we read verses like the following, it is puzzling.

I perceived that there is nothing better for them than to be joyful and to do good as long as they live; also that everyone should eat and drink and take pleasure in all his toil—this is God's gift to man.
ECCLESIASTES 3:12-13

*What I have seen to be good and fitting is to eat and drink and find enjoyment
in all the toil with which one toils under the sun the few days of his life that
God has given him, for this is his lot. Everyone also to whom God has given
wealth and possessions and power to enjoy them, and to accept his lot and
rejoice in his toil—this is the gift of God.*

ECCLESIASTES 5:18-19

*And I commend joy, for man has nothing better under the sun but to eat and
drink and be joyful, for this will go with him in his toil through the days of his
life that God has given him under the sun. Ecclesiastes 8:15*

ECCLESIASTES 8:15

The world is cursed, broken, and harsh. Ecclesiastes has reinforced this time and
again, yet we are commanded to take pleasure. Solomon commends joy to us.
We are told to enjoy what God has given us. It seems discordant.

**What is Ecclesiastes driving at by urging, even commanding, us to find joy
and pleasure in the midst of a broken down world where all is vanity?**

We must realize that the curse did not remove God's fingerprints from the world nor did
it diminish His sovereignty over it. No, creation is not utterly good the way it once was,
but it is still woven through with goodness. Nothing in creation ultimately fulfills, nothing
lasts forever, but God's creative brilliance and kindness is tangible everywhere we look.

**Where do you see and appreciate the goodness of God's creation?
What aspects of life and creation move you to gratitude and gladness?**

We've seen in previous sessions how Ecclesiastes lifts our eyes to see above the sun,
and moves us to push back the darkness of a fallen world. That is happening here
too, maybe even more explicitly.

**How does the command to take pleasure in God's creation and His good
gifts lift our eyes above the sun? How does it push back the darkness?**

Ecclesiastes

When Ecclesiastes calls us to enjoy God's good gifts it is actually recovering some of God's design that was broken at the fall. By rightly enjoying creation and being grateful we are reordering what has been in chaos. Under the sun, almost all enjoyment trends toward idolatry. We instinctively (sinfully) seek fulfillment and ultimate gratification through temporal things. So when we're commanded to eat bread and do work and enjoy loved ones with gratitude to God, it is anti-idolatry. It places the gifts and the giver in their proper places and turns our eyes to where true happiness lies.

How does grateful pleasure-seeking like this invite others into reality with God?

How can we take vain pleasure-seeking and turn it into grateful pleasure-seeking?

What areas of enjoyment and pleasure in your life might you need to make this switch?

This sort of enjoyment is loud in a world of anxious, hungry, empty seekers. People are dying for identity, fulfillment, and joy. And we can offer it, through Christ. We can model how to be free from manic pursuits and clamoring. Because we are grounded in the giver and because our hope lies above the sun in Jesus Christ, we can enjoy God's gifts with no pressure. And we can invite others into that freedom. Ecclesiastes shows how to both be deeply happy and how to change the lives of those around us.

Personal Study 3
Pleasure Above the Sun

Everything we looked at from Ecclesiastes in the first 5 sessions of this study focused on life under the sun. Session 6 quite literally brought that to its end. By focusing on Ecclesiastes' teaching on death we were crossing a boundary between life under the sun and life above the sun. In this session we've moved fully above the sun, at least in terms of our perspective. All the passages we've studied are aimed at life under the sun, but all the commands to take pleasure and find joy would be utter nonsense if they were rooted in vanity. They are rooted in reality above the sun and bring that reality to our daily lives.

We looked previously at how finding joy in God's gifts reflects Genesis 1 and the goodness of creation.

Read Ecclesiastes 3:15.

God seeks what has been driven away.
ECCLESIASTES 3:15

According to the verse above, what does God desire to accomplish?

We know from the whole story arc of Scripture that God is not seeking to go backward, so to "seek what has been driven away" doesn't mean that God wants to return to Eden and the way creation was. It does mean that He wants to restore the pure, unadulterated goodness of creation. How? Through the work of Jesus Christ.

How does the work of Jesus Christ restore the goodness of creation?

Ecclesiastes

Jesus Christ came to save sinners, and make us new creations (2 Corinthians 5:17). But it is a gross misunderstanding of the gospel, the whole good news of Christ, to think that is the entirety of His work. Jesus came to conquer sin and death, like we saw in the previous session. At the cross He did just that. How? Through the resurrection; when Jesus rose from the dead He was the "firstfruits" of the resurrection of the dead (1 Corinthians 15:20-21). He was undoing the curse of Genesis 3. And one day He will complete the undoing when He returns—He will usher in a new heavens and a new earth (Revelation 21:1). When Ecclesiastes says God "seeks what has been driven away" this is what it means.

> **How does the command to take pleasure in the good gifts of God point to the huge, conquering work of Jesus Christ?**

Let's backtrack now. How does taking pleasure in our bread and wine and loved ones and work connect to all this? It's pretty clear how they honor God, but what do they have to do with a new heaven and a new earth? Because doing so is setting things right side up. It is restoring creation's order. When we eat a burger with a smile and go for a beautiful hike with friends and close our eyes to soak up our favorite music we are reflecting creation the way God intended—His people relishing His good gifts with freedom, joy, and gratitude. Every time we find joy in a gift from God it reflects the goodness of heaven and shows "above the sun" reality to the world we inhabit.

> **Most of us think of evangelism or missions as things God calls us to in order to invite people into his kingdom. But what about joy and enjoyment? What might your life look like if you saw those as means of doing God's mission?**

Ecclesiastes is not merely giving us permission to enjoy life under the sun. It is giving us a cause, a mission. By seeking joy in the gifts of the Lord we are introducing the world around us to the reality of a new heaven and a new earth (Revelation 21:1-8).

It is a faint reflection, a mere echo. But in a world where all is vanity and people are grasping at anything and everything for purpose and fulfillment and direction and peace it is loud and beautiful.

How does this command to pursue enjoyment, and this idea of mission, affect your peace of mind? What might it do for you in times of trouble, worry, or anxiety?

In our own lives, obeying this command pushes back the darkness too. Ecclesiastes says of the one who finds enjoyment,

> *He will not much remember the days of his life because God keeps*
> *him occupied with joy in his heart.*
> **ECCLESIASTES 5:20**

This doesn't mean we will be in a stupor but rather that the painful, burdensome things will roll back and be diminished in the face of the joy God gives. So this means that when we face trials and hard seasons of life one of the remedies is to seek pleasure in the simple gifts of the Lord.

Practically speaking, what are ways you can seek pleasure in a way that honors the Lord?

You are called to eat and to drink and to dance and to laugh and to explore and to listen. You are called to create and appreciate and cook and learn. You are called to flourish and to relish God's good gifts. To do so is a taste of heaven, a reflection of Jesus's work, and a remedy to the darkness of life under the sun.

Fear God and Keep His Commands

Start

Use this section to get the conversation started.

How does one conclude a study on such a rich, deep, complex book? It would be difficult to recap all the ground we've covered. A few points of application would be too simplistic. So let's follow the example of the author, Solomon.

> *The end of the matter; all has been heard. Fear God and keep*
> *his commandments, for this is the whole duty of man.*
> **ECCLESIASTES 12:13**

How does this verse help us close and sum up such a complex book as Ecclesiastes?

This final charge to readers sounds simple, an easy list of instructions. But it is actually a comprehensive paradigm for life under the sun. It is a summation of all that it takes to navigate a complex, contentious, broken world. It is our road map, and our way forward. And it is the framework that allows us to make sense out of deep, complicated realities like the ones we have studied.

Think about the themes we've studied from Ecclesiastes—all is vanity under the sun, wisdom, work, wealth/fame/power, justice, death, enjoyment. How does this simple but deep verse help us navigate each one?

Watch

Take notes as you watch video session 8.

To access the teaching sessions,
use the instructions in the back
of your Bible study book.

Discuss

Use this section to guide your group discussion.

When we read "the end of the matter; all has been heard" we need to do so with care. This isn't some Porky Pig "that's all folks!" sign off. It isn't a simplistic closing statement to leave us with a word to think about. Rather, picture Solomon in his old age seeking to give a final, lasting word of wisdom to help his readers navigate life well. He has woven together 11 plus chapters of thematic wisdom and wants to close with something that will help us understand all of it, to summarize the message and instructions of Ecclesiastes.

How would you summarize Ecclesiastes? What would your final words about the book be to help people understand it?

And this is his summary, his closing instructions to wrap up the whole book: "fear God and keep His commandments, for this is the whole duty of man." That's it. So simple. So clear. Yet not at all small or cute or simplistic. This offers a paradigm for life, a shape into which every decision we make and direction we take must fit. Let's walk through it.

What does "fear God" mean? Why is it a good thing considering most fear is bad and most things we are afraid of are to be avoided?

"Fear God" is the foundation for these final words. This means to live with the awareness that God is real and is exactly who He says He is in the Bible. It means living as if God is sovereign over all things and good in all He does. It means being in awe of God and worshiping Him. And yes, it does mean being afraid, but not because God is capricious or unpredictable or has even the slightest hint of malice in Him. Rather it is a fear of wonder and respect because of His greatness and holiness. Think of Isaiah's response to seeing God, "woe is me, for I am man of unclean lips," or John's response in Revelation 1: "I fell at his feet as though dead."

Consider the command to "fear God." How does it reframe how you view God? What needs to change in your heart toward God?

What does fearing God do to how we view ourselves?

Fearing God shapes how we view ourselves and our lives. It orders things rightly, with God at the head and everything else falling into place behind and below. This is why "the fear of the Lord is the beginning of wisdom" (Proverbs 9:10). While fearing God keeps us from thinking too much of ourselves, it does not diminish how we see ourselves. Rather, fearing God helps us see the dignity and purpose and beauty of being an image-bearer. It aligns us with God, so when we read "and keep his commandments" it just fits. Of course we will obey the commands of this creator God, how could we not? His Word is our whole rule of life.

The final charge ends with "for this is the whole duty of man."

What does "the whole duty of man" mean?
What does fulfilling this duty look like?

To fear God and keep His commandments is everything we are called to—our purpose and direction. On the one hand, this is a simple command, but on the other hand this covers literally every aspect of life. It is a call to faithfulness (fear God) and holiness (keep his commandments). It means we are called to live under the sun like we are destined for eternity with God. Because in Christ, we are.

What difference would it make in this broken world if followers of Christ lived in this manner?

What better way to conclude Ecclesiastes than to, in no uncertain terms, lift our eyes above the sun in an explicit call to fear God! How else can we navigate this broken world under the sun? How else can we make wise decisions than fearing the Lord and keeping His commandments? After wading through a morass of complexities and tensions, we are left with clarity. It isn't easy and it is no quick fix, but to fear God and keep his commandments is to find our identity, our purpose, our direction, and our happiness even as we navigate life under the sun.

What is your biggest takeaway from our time in Ecclesiastes?

Close the session with prayer.

Personal Study 1
Guided Reading

During the next week read the following verses to gain a deeper appreciation for what Ecclesiastes teaches about living with God.

ECCLESIASTES 3:9-15

We looked at this passage earlier, focusing on a couple different aspects. This time take note of the sentence, "He has put eternity into man's heart." This is a profound statement in the midst of a book about things passing away; man is set apart as an image bearer in a unique way. But the passage also clarifies man's limitations: "yet so that he cannot find out what God has done from the beginning to the end." The passage goes on to highlight that what God does lasts forever. So we see here that God made man uniquely, packed with eternity and meaning, and God's works do not pass away.

ECCLESIASTES 5:1-7

These verses are a call to obedience and reverence, to remember God as we live under the sun. They tell us to guard our hearts and our actions because God is in heaven and we are on earth. He is the one we must obey and fear, not our dreams or desires.

ECCLESIASTES 8:10-13

This passage highlights the value of waiting on the Lord and trusting Him. It often appears like the wicked are prospering in life because God's judgments do not come as swiftly as we would like, but it will be well for those who fear God and go poorly for those who don't. God will set things right in the end.

ECCLESIASTES 11–12

Chapters 11–12 turn our attention fully above the sun. The prior chapters focused primarily on navigating life under the sun in a manner that honored God, but these chapters focus more clearly on reality with God. They emphasize His sovereignty and working of mysteries that are beyond our understanding. They call on us to remember our creator, and there is a sense of urgency because life under the sun is short. In summary and conclusion, the passage tells us that Solomon offered words of knowledge, wisdom, delight, and truth—a good way to think about the whole of Ecclesiastes. And it concludes with "Fear God and keep His commandments, for this is the whole duty of man." This is a banner over the whole book.

Notes

Personal Study 2

Fear the Lord

When you read "Fear God and keep his commandments" it reads like a list: "first do this, then do this." That would be problematic for us, though, because it would shift the weight of obedience onto our willpower and strength which would set us up for burnout and failure. A better way to understand this command would be "keep God's commandments *because* you fear Him."

How is fearing God a motivation to obey Him?

What is it about God that motivates you to obey Him?

What makes obeying God's commands so difficult sometimes?

When we fear God, obedience is the result, not a thing we decide to do in addition. Fearing God means reflecting on all He is, all He has done, and living in that reality. If we are doing that, how could we not be moved to obedience?

Fear is a terrible long-term motivation. How is fearing the Lord different? What makes it healthy rather than costly and diminishing for us?

One objection that stares us right in the face is that fear is a terrible long-term motivator in almost any relational circumstance. If I, as a dad, make a habit out of using scare tactics and intimidation to get my kids to obey, it might work in the sense that they do the things I command. But I will lose their affection, drive them away, and as they grow and gain independence they will likely rebel and resent me. Why is fearing God any different? In what sense is fearing the Lord a good motivation for obedience?

Remember, fearing God is not built on terror or intimidation. God is not bullying us into obedience with strength and sheer force of will. Our fear for Him is worship, wonder, awe, and deep realization that He is utterly Holy and we are not. Fear of God does not forget that He is "slow to anger and abounding in steadfast love" (Exodus 34:6). There is plenty of reason to be afraid of God, but not for those who fear Him. Ecclesiastes says:

> It will be well with those who fear God, because they fear before him.
> But it will not be well with the wicked.
> **ECCLESIASTES 8:12-13**

The wicked are those who don't take God seriously, those who rebel, those who do not fear Him—and they should be afraid. Those who fear God have nothing to fear.

Throughout Ecclesiastes we've seen evidence of God's kindness under the sun. And like so many other themes in the book, these references are there to lift our eyes to a better reality and help us see the goodness and grace of God. Fearing the Lord means taking in His whole character, and the heart of God is shaped by love and grace. He is marked by patience and mercy.

How would focusing on God's grace change your willingness to obey?

How would it change your joy in obeying?

Consider the words of Jesus:

> For God so loved the world, that he gave his only Son, that whoever believes in him should not perish but have eternal life. For God did not send his Son into the world to condemn the world, but in order that the world might be saved through him.
> **JOHN 3:16-17**

These verses are the heart of God and how He showed it! God's wrath is not His primary posture or His inclination; it's a necessary and just response to evil in order to protect and uphold what is holy and right and to protect the ones He loves.

So what motivates us to obey? The love and smile of our Father. "Fear God and keep his commandments" has a built-in promise of peace and happiness. Under the sun we won't have ease, but if we are with God all will be well for us.

How does fearing the Lord lead to wisdom, and why is this so important for life under the sun?

When have you experiencing the wisdom that comes from fearing the Lord?

Solomon said elsewhere:

> *The fear of the Lord is the beginning of wisdom.*
> **PROVERBS 9:10**

So if we live a life marked by reverence, awe, gratitude, and obedience to God we will be well-positioned to navigate this murky, messy, complex, complicated life under the sun. As we focus our attention on God and orient our lives around Him we will be able to weigh difficult decisions, we will reflect His values when situations are not either/or, and we will proceed with His character shaping us. We will live with our eyes above the sun as we live under it.

Consider Psalm 107:43.

> *Whoever is wise, let him attend to these things; let them consider*
> *the steadfast love of the LORD.*
> **PSALM 107:43**

The fear of the Lord is the beginning of wisdom, and the wise ones will consider and meditate on the steadfast love of the Lord. How can your life reflect these foundational, shaping realities?

Personal Study 3

The Whole Duty of Man

Read the final words of Ecclesiastes again.

> *The end of the matter; all has been heard. Fear God and keep*
> *his commandments, for this is the whole duty of man.*
> **ECCLESIASTES 12:13**

What does Ecclesiastes mean by "this is the whole duty of man?"

When we hear "duty" we likely think of something work-related or maybe we think of the police or the military who we expect to fulfill their duties. Is that what Ecclesiastes is talking about as it closes? Is it giving us a task list, our marching orders? That would be out of character for a book that has been much more about reorienting and reprioritizing our hearts and minds than about giving us lists of rules. Moreover, it would be heavy-handed.

> **If we understood "whole duty of man" to be our responsibility, our task list, how**
> **could we achieve this? Why would this be a poor way to understand this verse?**

What chance would sinners like you or I have to fulfill this duty? By nature we don't fear God. Even at our best we only partially obey God's commandments. We are "by nature children of wrath" (Ephesians 2:3) outside of Christ's saving mercy. So either Ecclesiastes is leaving us high and dry, or it is keeping in character and calling us to something infinitely better than mere will-powered obedience.

> **What is this "whole duty of man" calling us to? How is it reframing and**
> **reorienting our perspective toward something eternally good?**

Ecclesiastes

Ecclesiastes is a book about Jesus, or at least a book that shows the world's profound need for Jesus. And its conclusion is maybe the clearest signpost pointing to Christ. Who in the history of the world has ever perfectly feared God and kept His commandments? Only Jesus. Only Jesus has fulfilled the whole duty of man.

Reflect on the person and life of Christ. How did he fulfill this whole duty?

While it wouldn't be theologically correct to say Jesus "feared God" because that means that God is above the one doing the fearing, and Jesus said "I and the Father are one" (John 10:30), Jesus did honor God the Father perfectly in all He said and did (John 17:4-5). He lived, as a man, in a manner that showed what fearing the Lord perfectly looks like. Jesus was "tempted as we are, yet without sin" (Hebrews 4:15). He obeyed the commandments of God perfectly. In short, Jesus fulfilled the whole duty of man.

What difference does it make for us that Jesus fulfilled the whole duty of man?

This is the good news of the gospel. That's right, Ecclesiastes points to the gospel! Jesus fulfilled what we could not, he lived a perfect life so that He could be the flawless sacrifice for our sins and satisfy the justice of God. (And remember John 3:16-17, Jesus came as the will and plan of God; they were in it together to save us.) He made a way for us to be right in the eyes of God, to be declared innocent of our sins, to be justified. And what is more, he opened the door for relationship with God. Whereas we couldn't be in God's holy presence without Jesus (Romans 3:23), if we are in Christ God looks at us and sees the righteousness and perfection of His Son.

In light of the work of Jesus, how does "Fear God and keep His commandments, for this is the whole duty of man" strike you? How does Jesus change things?

So when we read "Fear God and keep His commandments, for this is the whole duty of man" it shouldn't land on us like a demand we can't fulfill but as an invitation to give ourselves to Jesus Christ. What's more, all those who believe in Christ have the Holy Spirit living in us as our teacher, helper, guide, convicter, and wisdom (Romans 8:9). So not only did Christ fulfill the whole duty of Man, He sent the Spirit, His very presence, to enable us to grow in doing the same.

Conclusion

Ecclesiastes is wisdom literature, aimed at shaping our minds and hearts in fear of the Lord and honoring Him as we navigate life under the sun. As we've seen, it primarily does that by exploring what is broken and then pointing to the eternal hope and solution: reality with God and life with Christ.

When Solomon wrote these words he did not know of Jesus, but He believed in Jesus—the coming redeemer. We have a remarkable advantage in that we have the rest of the story. We know of the incarnation, the crucifixion, the resurrection, the ascension, and the promise that Jesus will return to set things right and make all things new. All our hope lies in these truths!

But we still live under the sun. We live in a broken world where "all is vanity." This side of heaven, our hearts will tug us toward idolatry, toward seeking purpose and fulfillment and happiness in things that will not last and will not ultimately deliver. So we need the realistic wisdom of this book to set our expectations, reframe our perspective, reorient our hearts, and to help us "set our minds on things that are above, not on things that are on earth" (Colossians 3:2).

What a remarkable gift to have these grounded, blunt truths to shake us from our earthly stupor and to be able to read them in light of the gospel of Jesus Christ as our true and full hope. Now, under the smile of God and in the truth of the gospel,

> *Go, eat your bread with joy, and drink your wine with a merry heart, for God has already approved what you do. Let your garments be always white. Let not oil be lacking on your head. Enjoy life with the wife whom you love, all the days of your vain life that he has given you under the sun, because that is your portion in life and in your toil at which you toil under the sun. Whatever your hand finds to do, do it with your might.*
> **ECCLESIASTES 9:7-10A**

Ecclesiastes

Leader Guide

Tips for Leading a Small Group

Follow these guidelines to prepare for each group session.

Prayerfully Prepare

REVIEW. Review the weekly material and group questions ahead of time.

PRAY. Be intentional about praying for each person in the group. Ask the Holy Spirit to work through you and the group discussion as you point to Jesus each week through God's Word.

Minimize Distractions

Create a comfortable environment. If group members are uncomfortable, they'll be distracted and therefore not engaged in the group experience. Plan ahead by considering these details, include seating, temperature, lighting, food and drink, and general cleanliness. Do everything in your ability to help people focus on what's most important: connecting with God, with the Bible, and with one another.

Encourage Discussion

A good small group experience has the following characteristics.

EVERYONE IS INCLUDED. Your goal is to foster a community in which people are welcome just as they are but encouraged to grow spiritually. Always be aware of opportunities to include any people who visit the group and to invite new people to join your group.

EVERYONE PARTICIPATES. Encourage everyone to ask questions, share responses, or read aloud.

NO ONE DOMINATES—NOT EVEN THE LEADER. Be sure that your time speaking as a leader takes up less than half of your time together as a group. Politely guide discussion if anyone dominates.

NOBODY IS RUSHED THROUGH QUESTIONS. Don't feel that a moment of silence is a bad thing. People often need time to think about their responses to questions they've just heard or to gain courage to share what God is stirring in their hearts.

INPUT IS AFFIRMED AND FOLLOWED UP. Make sure you point out something true or helpful in a response. Don't just move on. Build community with follow-up questions, asking how other people have experienced similar things or how a truth has shaped their understanding of God and the Scripture you're studying. People are less likely to speak up if they fear that you don't actually want to hear their answers or that you're looking for only a certain answer.

GOD AND HIS WORD ARE CENTRAL. Opinions and experiences can be helpful, but God has given us the truth. Trust God's Word to be the authority and God's Spirit to work in people's lives. You can't change anyone, but God can. Continually point people to the Word and to active steps of faith.

Keep Connecting

Think of ways to connect with group members during the week. Participation during the group session is always improved when members spend time connecting with one another outside the group sessions. The more people are comfortable with and involved in one another's lives, the more they'll look forward to being together. When people move beyond being friendly to truly being friends who form a community, they come to each session eager to engage instead of merely attending.

Encourage group members with thoughts, commitments, or questions from the session by connecting through texts, calls, and emails.

When possible, build deeper friendships by planning or spontaneously inviting group members to join you outside your regularly scheduled group time for activities, meals, group hangouts, or projects around your home, church, or community.

Session 1
Vanity Under the Sun

Before the Session

1. Review the group content as well as the video teaching session.
2. Read and review the passages of Ecclesiastes included in the *Guided Reading* section to prepare yourself for the group discussion.
3. Read through the *Reading Wisdom Literature* section.
4. Decide whether you're going to watch the video teaching sessions together or if you want group members to watch them prior to the group meeting. Each book includes codes to access the video teaching. Each video is 10-15 minutes long.
5. Pray for all group members by name.
6. Review the questions in the *Start* and *Discuss* sections and adjust as needed.

During the Session

1. Highlight the main point. "Vanity under the sun" is the main theme as well as the context of Ecclesiastes. Be sure to define both.
2. Vanity In Ecclesiastes is not meaninglessness. Rather it refers to the fading, temporal nature of our experience in this life. It means that nothing functions the way it should and that nothing we experience will be as fulfilling as we hoped it would be.
3. Under the sun is a location and a duration. A location—the entire earth. A duration—the span of our lives in a fallen world awaiting redemption in Christ.
4. Be sure to point out how Jesus gives purpose and meaning to our lives of vanity under the sun. Other sessions will highlight this more fully, but we want to get group members thinking about this truth from the beginning of the study.
5. Explain the remaining sections of each session—Guided Reading and Personal Study 1 and 2. Remind them to complete all three prior to the next meeting. Encourage them to complete the Guided Reading before the sessions. This will give them the best opportunity to truly interact with the material.
6. Close in prayer.
7. Remind them to complete the Guided Reading and Personal Studies before the next meeting.

After the Session

Consider meeting in groups of two or three to discuss and review the guided reading. Here are a few questions to ask during that time. Alternately, you might consider sending these questions to the group in a text or email to consider on their own.

> **How does the opening section of Ecclesiastes prepare us for the tone and message of the book?**
>
> **How did the framework of "under the sun" offer clarity in understanding "all is vanity"?**
>
> **After the group session, how much easier was it to identity the theme and context of Ecclesiastes in your reading?**
>
> **What reasons for hope did you uncover in your reading?**

Prayer

Pray that group members would truly grasp the theme of vanity under the sun.

Ask that the Holy Spirit would give them His understanding of this book of Scripture.

Ask that God would use your group's time in this study to change your lives and mold your group together and individually into the image of His Son, Jesus.

Session 2
Wisdom

Before the Session

1. Review the group content as well as the video teaching session.
2. Read and review the passages of Ecclesiastes included in the *Guided Reading* section to prepare yourself for the group discussion.
3. Pray for all group members by name.
4. Review the questions in the *Start* and *Discuss* sections and adjust as needed.
5. Prepare a few takeaways from your personal study to share in the *Start* section.

During the Session

1. Review the previous week using the *Start* section.
2. Highlight the definition of wisdom that Barnabas gives in the video teaching: living life with godly skill, thinking with the mind of God, and prioritizing or judging with godly priorities.
3. Point out that when Ecclesiastes refers to wisdom as vanity, it is not saying wisdom is useless or pointless. Solomon is saying that wisdom in a fallen world is limited in use and effectiveness.
4. Remind the group that despite the limitations of wisdom in a fallen world, it is still worth pursuing.
5. State that for Christians, Jesus is both the wisdom and power of God (1 Corinthians 1:24).
6. Close in prayer.
7. Remind them to complete the Guided Reading and Personal Studies before the next meeting.

After the Session

Consider meeting in groups of two or three to discuss and review the guided reading. Here are a few questions to ask during that time. Alternately, you might consider sending these questions to the group in a text or email to consider on their own.

What unique qualification did Solomon have that made him an adept guide to help us understand the limits of wisdom?

What teaching on wisdom from the reading did you find most helpful? Most confusing? Most necessary in today's world?

What are some ways we can pursue wisdom and avoid what the Bible calls "foolishness"?

Prayer

Thank Jesus for being the wisdom and power of God for all who believe.

Ask that God would help the group to see the value and necessity of godly wisdom.

Pray that the group would also see the limits of wisdom and that in seeing the limits of wisdom they would turn to and trust God more fully.

Session 3

Work

Before the Session

1. Review the group content as well as the video teaching session.
2. Read and review the passages of Ecclesiastes included in the *Guided Reading* section to prepare yourself for the group discussion.
3. Pray for all group members by name.
4. Review the questions in the *Start* and *Discuss* sections and adjust as needed.
5. Prepare a few takeaways from your personal study to share in the *Start* section.

During the Session

1. Review the previous week using the *Start* section.
2. Be aware of the ways work and career shape the lives of the people in your group.
3. Keep in mind that many people view work in a spectrum between two poles. Some look to work for their purpose and identity in life while others see work as unfulfilling toil. The biblical understanding of work falls somewhere in the middle.
4. According to the Scriptures, work is a blessing from God given before the fall but because of the fall we can be tempted to receive ultimate fulfillment or no fulfillment at all from our work. We need to put work in its proper context.
5. Remind the group that rest is a God-given counterbalance to work. We need rest just as much as work.
6. Point out that Jesus gives us the ability to work for His sake (Colossians 3:23-24).
7. Close in prayer.
8. Remind them to complete the Guided Reading and Personal Studies before the next meeting.

After the Session

Consider meeting in groups of two or three to discuss and review the guided reading. Here are a few questions to ask during that time. Alternately, you might consider sending these questions to the group in a text or email to consider on their own.

Based on the reading in Ecclesiastes, how do you need to adjust your understand of work?

Do you maintain a healthy balance between rest and work? If not, what needs to change?

What joy could you find in your work? How might finding joy in work keep it from becoming and idol or an annoyance?

Prayer

Pray that group members would develop a biblical framework for viewing work.

Ask the Holy Spirit to help us avoid extremes in how we view our work.

Pray that we would all use our skills, influence, and careers to further the work of Christ in the world.

Session 4
Wealth, Fame, and Power

Before the Session

1. Review the group content as well as the video teaching session.
2. Read and review the passages of Ecclesiastes included in the *Guided Reading* section to prepare yourself for the group discussion.
3. Pray for all group members by name.
4. Review the questions in the *Start* and *Discuss* sections and adjust as needed.
5. Prepare a few takeaways from your personal study to share in the *Start* section.

During the Session

1. Point out that this session is closely connected with the previous study.
2. Unless they are very self-aware, understand that many in your group will not feel that wealth, fame, and power are problems with which they struggle. Help them see that all of us struggle with wealth, fame, and power in a variety of ways.
3. Highlight that wealth, fame, and power are often associated with pride and ego. Perhaps rightly so, however, point out that all of these things can be an effective tool for God's kingdom when used by a person filled with biblical wisdom.
4. Help the group see that being tempted by wealth, fame, and power are more common struggles than they may initially think, but like every other struggle, they can be handed over to God.
5. State that in His earthly ministry, Jesus was a renowned teacher, followed by crowds. In Jesus, we see a model of how to steward fame and influence with God-exalting humility and wisdom.
6. Close in prayer.
7. Remind them to complete the Guided Reading and Personal Studies before the next meeting.

After the Session

Consider meeting in groups of two or three to discuss and review the guided reading. Here are a few questions to ask during that time. Alternately, you might consider sending these questions to the group in a text or email to consider on their own.

Solomon, the author of Ecclesiastes, was a man of power and influence. How did he squander that notoriety? What can we learn from his example?

How does Ecclesiastes 4 help us put our gifts into perspective? What influence do you have? How are you using it?

How do these verses reshape the way you think about wealth, fame, and power?

Prayer

Pray that group members would have the supernatural ability to see how wealth, fame, and power are impacting their lives.

Thank God for the wealth, fame, and power that we've been given. Ask that He would help us steward them well.

Above all else, pray that we would seek to make Jesus known and famous instead of ourselves. Like John the Baptist said, we must decrease, He must increase.

Session 5
Justice

Before the Session

1. Review the group content as well as the video teaching session.
2. Read and review the passages of Ecclesiastes included in the *Guided Reading* section to prepare yourself for the group discussion.
3. Pray for all group members by name.
4. Review the questions in the *Start* and *Discuss* sections and adjust as needed.
5. Prepare a few takeaways from your personal study to share in the *Start* section.

During the Session

1. Going in, realize that "justice" is a particularly fraught word these days. However, it is a biblical ideal that merits our time and consideration. Try to keep the conversation on track by limiting it to what is discussed in the group session.
2. Keep in mind that Ecclesiastes addresses justice by broadly pointing out the inequity and pain caused by living in a fallen world. Solomon speaks of the kind of injustice that all see and feel.
3. Help them to see that as with many ideas in Ecclesiastes, the book is trying to paint a bleak backdrop against which "above the sun" reality can shine.
4. Point out that injustice is only temporary. There is a day coming soon when God will right every wrong and make every bad thing untrue. Until that day we wait with hope and expectation.
5. Close in prayer.
6. Remind them to complete the Guided Reading and Personal Studies before the next meeting.

After the Session

Consider meeting in groups of two or three to discuss and review the guided reading. Here are a few questions to ask during that time. Alternately, you might consider sending these questions to the group in a text or email to consider on their own.

How does Ecclesiastes help us see the inequity and unfairness of life under the sun? Why is this a good thing?

How does Ecclesiastes portray death as a great evil but also a great leveler?

How do these passages point us to reality above the sun?

Prayer

Pray that group members would long for the kind of justice that only Jesus can provide.

Ask the Holy Spirit to strengthen us as we live in a world that is marked by injustice rather than justice.

Pray that we would be motivated to seek justice so far as it depends on us.

Session 6
Number Your Days

Before the Session

1. Review the group content as well as the video teaching session.
2. Read and review the passages of Ecclesiastes included in the *Guided Reading* section to prepare yourself for the group discussion.
3. Pray for all group members by name.
4. Review the questions in the *Start* and *Discuss* sections and adjust as needed.
5. Prepare a few takeaways from your personal study to share in the *Start* section.

During the Session

1. Realize that this week is about mortality and death and that not everyone will feel comfortable discussing these topics, so be gracious.
2. Point out that, like in the example from *What about Bob?,* many people avoid serious topics with deflection and humor. Ecclesiastes offers a better and more grounded alternative.
3. Help the group to see that death is a reoccurring theme in Ecclesiastes and really throughout the whole Bible.
4. Remember that while death is the stop button on life under the sun, it is not the final reality for Christians. Those who know Jesus have a truer and better reality to look forward to above the sun beyond this life.
5. Close in prayer.
6. Remind them to complete the Guided Reading and Personal Studies before the next meeting.

After the Session

Consider meeting in groups of two or three to discuss and review the guided reading. Here are a few questions to ask during that time. Alternately, you might consider sending these questions to the group in a text or email to consider on their own.

How does Ecclesiastes 3:1-8 give us context to the fading nature of life under the sun?

How does Ecclesiastes give us the wisdom to live well, knowing that our days are numbered?

What should the universal nature of death teach us about life under the sun? What does it teach us about the hope of heaven?

Prayer

Pray that group members would make the most of their days under the sun.

Ask that reflecting on death would not make us sullen or afraid but would instead encourage us to seek the reality above the sun.

Thank God for providing Jesus. Praise Him for His victory over death and the grave and the life we will share with Him in eternity.

Session 7

Enjoy the Life God has Given You

Before the Session

1. Review the group content as well as the video teaching session.
2. Read and review the passages of Ecclesiastes included in the *Guided Reading* section to prepare yourself for the group discussion.
3. Pray for all group members by name.
4. Review the questions in the *Start* and *Discuss* sections and adjust as needed.
5. Prepare a few takeaways from your personal study to share in the *Start* section.
6. Since this is the second to last week of the study, if this is an ongoing group, consider what your group will be doing next.

During the Session

1. Keep in mind that the ideas in this session might be new to people. Surely they enjoy good things in life, but they might not have ever considered how those things should point them to God.
2. Remind the group that the key to enjoying God's good gifts is gratitude. Being grateful for the things we have been given keeps us from seeing God's gifts as ultimate things.
3. Assure the group it is okay, even commanded, to enjoy good things from God.
4. Make sure that the group realizes that Jesus enjoyed life. He was invited to weddings and parties. He had friendships. We're told that the Son of Man came eating and drinking. Jesus shows us how to enjoy God's gifts as a way of enjoying God.
5. Close in prayer.
6. Remind them to complete the Guided Reading and Personal Studies before the next meeting.

After the Session

Consider meeting in groups of two or three to discuss and review the guided reading. Here are a few questions to ask during that time. Alternately, you might consider sending these questions to the group in a text or email to consider on their own.

For such a somber book, what can Ecclesiastes teach us about pleasure and joy?

How can the things we enjoy point us to reality above the sun?

Why should we not feel guilty about taking pleasure in the good gifts God has given us?

Prayer

Thank God for the good gifts that He gives.

Pray that the good gifts God has given us would point us toward Him and not rob our hearts away from Him.

Ask God to show you how you can help or bless someone else with the good gifts He has given you.

Session 8

Fear God and Keep His Commands

Before the Session

1. Review the group content as well as the video teaching session.
2. Read and review the passages of Ecclesiastes included in the *Guided Reading* section to prepare yourself for the group discussion.
3. Pray for all group members by name.
4. Review the questions in the *Start* and *Discuss* sections and adjust as needed.
5. Prepare a few takeaways from your personal study to share in the *Start* section.

During the Session

1. Make sure everyone in the group understands what it means to fear God. Those without a church background might be confused by the term. To fear God is to revere and worship Him for who He is.
2. Help the group to see that we come to know God more fully by obeying Him. When God commands our obedience, it is for our good and leads us into true and lasting life.
3. Remind the group that Jesus fully obeyed God and to be like Jesus is to obey. Also remind them that because Jesus obeyed, those who trust in Him have Jesus's obedience and faithfulness credited to them as righteousness.
4. Close in prayer.
5. Thank the group for participating and let them know what is coming next.

After the Session

Consider meeting in groups of two or three to discuss and review the guided reading. Here are a few questions to ask during that time. Alternately, you might consider sending these questions to the group in a text or email to consider on their own.

Why is it significant that "fear God and keep His commands" are Solomon's parting words in Ecclesiastes?

What does it look like to fear God and keep His commands in our daily life?

What's your biggest takeaway from our time in Ecclesiastes?

Prayer

Thank God for the time you had as a group in Ecclesiastes. Ask Him to use the experiencing to conform you into the image of His Son.

Pray that this study would lead to a deeper and fuller understanding of Ecclesiastes.

Ask that as a result of this time that you would all fear God and keep His commands.

DO YOU EVER DOUBT GOD?

The Bible says that we can only grasp spiritual things as we see a poor reflection in a mirror. Such a poor understanding will often create doubt. But God is not surprised. In fact, He welcomes your doubt because it's often the beginning of a deeper, stronger relationship with Him. This new Bible study will help you see that faith is a process of learning all we can understand about God and trusting Him in all we can't. Learn more online or call 800.458.2772.

lifeway.com/helpmyunbelief

Lifeway

What happens when heaven touches earth?

When Jesus came to earth, he chose John as one of His closest friends. This Bible study examines the first three chapters of John's account of this remarkable time in history and the eternal implications for us all. You may think you know about Jesus, but you're going to learn something new. And you just might fall in love with Him all over again, or maybe for the first time.

Lifeway

Everything is futile?

At first glance, the book of Ecclesiastes paints a bleak picture. But is life really as empty and meaningless as Solomon seems to suggest?

Ecclesiastes offers a gritty look at how hard life can be, but it also points to where hope can be found in the midst of it. Yes, there are times when we suffer. There are times when things don't make sense. But if we lift our eyes, we can see the truth that's better than this life we live, and it's found in Christ.

This eight-session Bible study will help you:

- Learn that Jesus is our wisdom—the way we can live wisely and find happiness.
- Get a biblical perspective on God, life, pleasure, and mortality.
- View your earthly pursuits from God's perspective.
- Better understand the book of Ecclesiastes.